Small Habits, Big Rewards - A Step-by-Step Guide to Financial
Freedom

Nathan Brooks - 2023

# Table of Contents:

# Introduction

Have you ever found yourself struggling to get your finances in order? Do you feel like no matter how hard you try; you can't seem to break free from debt and achieve financial freedom? If so, you're not alone. Many people today are living paycheck to paycheck, drowning in debt, and feeling like they have no control over their financial future.

But what if I told you that you could achieve financial freedom by focusing on small, simple habits that you can incorporate into your daily life? These are micro habits – tiny actions that might seem insignificant on their own, but when practiced consistently, can have a huge impact on your financial well-being.

This book is all about helping you develop these micro habits for financial freedom. We'll start by exploring the importance of mindset – how the way you think about money can impact your financial success. We'll then dive into specific micro habits you can implement to improve your finances, organized into categories such as budgeting, saving, investing, and more.

But why micro habits? Why focus on small, seemingly insignificant actions rather than big, sweeping changes? The truth is that big changes can be overwhelming and hard to sustain. They require a lot of willpower, and when we inevitably slip up, it's easy to feel like we've failed and give up altogether.

Micro habits, on the other hand, are easy to incorporate into your daily routine. They don't require a lot of effort or willpower, and they can be practiced consistently without feeling overwhelming. And while each individual habit might not seem like it's making a huge impact on your finances, when you add them up over time, they can lead to significant progress.

Take, for example, the habit of bringing your lunch to work instead of eating out. It might seem like a small change, but if you do it every day, you could save hundreds of dollars over the course of a year. And if you then take that money and put it towards paying off debt or investing, the impact becomes even greater.

Another example is tracking your expenses. This might seem tedious, but by simply writing down everything you spend, you become more aware of where your money is going. You might notice patterns or areas where you're overspending, which can then lead to making changes in your budget and saving more money.

The key to success with micro habits is consistency. It's not about making huge changes overnight – it's about making small changes that you can sustain over time. When you consistently practice these habits, they become part of your daily routine and you start to see the impact on your finances.

Of course, developing new habits is easier said than done. It's easy to fall back into old patterns, especially when it comes to money. That's why this book is designed to help you not only identify the micro habits that can improve your finances, but also provide tips and strategies for making those habits stick.

Throughout the book, you'll find real-life examples of people who have successfully implemented micro habits for financial freedom. You'll also find exercises and prompts to help you apply the concepts to your own life, as well as additional resources for learning more about personal finance and developing good financial habits.

At the end of the day, achieving financial freedom isn't about getting rich quick or making huge sacrifices. It's about developing a mindset of abundance, practicing good financial habits consistently, and making small changes that add up over time. This book is your guide to developing those micro habits and taking control of your financial future.

# Chapter 1 – Budgeting and Expense Tracking

Effective budgeting is the foundation of sound financial management, and it is a skill that everyone should strive to develop. Whether you are trying to save money, pay off debt, or simply live within your means, a well-designed budget is essential.

In this chapter, we will explore the concept of budgeting in detail and explain why it is crucial for achieving your financial goals. We will also delve into the process of expense tracking and why it is a necessary component of budgeting. We will talk about the importance of budgeting and how it can help you take control of your finances. We will discuss the various benefits of creating a budget and why it is essential to track your expenses. We will also touch on the different types of budgets and the best practices for creating an effective one that suits your individual needs.

Expense tracking has also an important role in budgeting. We will explain why it is crucial to keep track of your expenses and how to do it effectively. We will explore the different methods of expense tracking, including manual and automated methods, and provide tips on how to choose the right method for you. Additionally, we will discuss the importance of categorizing your expenses and how to create an expense tracker that is easy to use and maintain.

By the end of this chapter, you will have a solid understanding of the importance of budgeting and expense tracking, and how they can help you achieve your financial goals. You will have learned various techniques for creating a budget that works for you, including the different types of budgets and best practices for creating one. You will also have gained valuable insights into the process of expense tracking, including the importance of categorizing your expenses and choosing the right tracking method for your lifestyle. Armed with this knowledge, you will be well on your way to taking control of your finances and building a strong foundation for your financial future.

Get an overview of your finances.

Before you can start making progress towards financial freedom, it is essential to get a clear overview of your current financial situation. This includes taking a look at your income, expenses, assets, and debts. Once you have a solid understanding of where you stand financially, you can begin to make informed decisions about how to move forward.

To get started, you'll need to gather all the necessary information. This includes your bank statements, credit card statements, and any other financial documents you have. You'll also need to make a list of all your income sources, including your salary, any bonuses, and any additional income you receive.

Next, it's time to take a look at your expenses. This includes everything from your monthly bills to your weekly grocery shopping trips. Start by creating a budget that includes all of your regular expenses. Be sure to include any annual or quarterly expenses as well, such as insurance premiums or property taxes.

Once you have a budget in place, it's time to take a closer look at your spending habits. This can be a bit overwhelming, but it's important to be honest with yourself about where your money is going. Start by tracking your expenses for a few weeks or even a month. This can help you identify any areas where you might be overspending or where you can cut back.

It's also important to take a look at your debts. Make a list of all your outstanding debts, including credit card balances, student loans, and any other loans you have. Be sure to include the interest rate and minimum payment for each debt. This will give you a clear picture of how much you owe and how much interest you're paying each month.

Once you have a clear understanding of your income, expenses, and debts, it's time to start making some changes. Begin by looking for ways to reduce your expenses. This might include things like canceling subscriptions you don't use or switching to a cheaper cell phone plan. Every little bit helps, and even small changes can add up over time.

Next, it's time to take a closer look at your debts. If you have credit card balances or other high-interest debts, consider consolidating them into a lower-interest loan. This can help you save money on interest and make it easier to pay off your debts.

Finally, it's important to start thinking about your long-term financial goals. This might include things like saving for a down payment on a house, paying off your student loans, or saving for retirement. Whatever your goals may be, it's important to start working towards them now.

One of the best ways to stay on track is to create a financial plan. This can help you identify your goals and map out a plan for achieving them. It's also important to revisit your plan regularly and make adjustments as needed. Life is unpredictable, and your financial situation can change at any time. By staying flexible and adaptable, you'll be better equipped to handle whatever comes your way.

In conclusion, getting an overview of your finances is an essential step towards achieving financial freedom. By taking the time to gather all the necessary information, creating a budget, and tracking your expenses, you'll have a solid understanding of your current financial situation. From there, you can start making changes to reduce your expenses, pay off your debts, and work towards your long-term financial goals. Remember, achieving financial freedom is a journey, not a destination. By taking small steps each day, you'll be well on your way to a brighter financial future.

## Set a daily budget.

Setting a daily budget is an essential step in achieving financial freedom. It's a way to ensure that your spending aligns with your income and goals, while also helping you to avoid overspending and accumulating unnecessary debt.

To set a daily budget, you need to start by understanding your current spending habits. You can do this by tracking your expenses for a week or two. This will give you an idea of how much you're spending on different categories such as food, transportation, housing, and entertainment.

Once you have an understanding of your current spending habits, you can begin to create a budget. Start by identifying your sources of income, including your salary, any side hustles, or any other sources of income. Next, you need to subtract your fixed expenses, such as rent or mortgage payments, utility bills, and any other monthly payments. This will give you an idea of how much disposable income you have each month.

To set a daily budget, divide your disposable income by the number of days in the month. For example, if you have $1,500 of disposable income each month and there are 30 days in the month, your daily budget would be $50. This means that you have $50 each day to spend on things like food, transportation, and entertainment.

It's important to remember that your daily budget isn't set in stone. It's okay to adjust your budget as needed, especially if unexpected expenses come up. If you overspend one day, try to cut back on your spending the following day to balance things out.

One way to help you stick to your daily budget is to use cash for your daily expenses. Withdraw your daily budget in cash each day and only use that cash for your expenses. This can help you avoid overspending and keep you accountable to your budget.

Another helpful tool is to use a budgeting app. There are many free budgeting apps available that can help you track your expenses and stick to your budget. Some popular options include Mint, Personal Capital, and YNAB.

Setting a daily budget isn't just about restricting your spending. It's also about prioritizing your spending and making sure that you're spending your money on things that matter to you. This means that you need to be intentional about your spending and make sure that your daily expenses align with your values and goals.

For example, if your goal is to save for a down payment on a house, you may need to cut back on your daily expenses, such as eating out or buying coffee. Instead, you can bring your own lunch to work and make coffee at home. By cutting back on these small expenses, you can save more money each day and put that money towards your savings goals.

In conclusion, setting a daily budget is an important step in achieving financial freedom. It helps you to understand your current spending habits and make intentional decisions about your money. By tracking your expenses, setting a budget, and sticking to it, you can make sure that your spending aligns with your income and goals. Remember, your daily budget isn't set in stone, and it's okay to adjust it as needed. By being intentional with your spending and making sure that your daily expenses align with your values and goals, you can achieve financial freedom and live the life you want.

Track your expenses.

When it comes to achieving financial freedom, tracking your expenses is an essential step. Knowing where your money goes is the key to understanding your spending habits and making informed decisions about your finances. It's easy to overspend when you don't keep track of your expenses, and before you know it, you're wondering where all your money went. However, by tracking your expenses, you can avoid this common pitfall and make sure you're using your money wisely.

Why Track Your Expenses?

There are several reasons why you should track your expenses. Firstly, it helps you identify where your money is going. This information is crucial because it allows you to see if you're spending too much money on certain things or if there are areas where you can cut back. It also helps you create a more accurate budget, as you can see how much you're spending in different categories and adjust your budget accordingly.

Secondly, tracking your expenses helps you stay on top of your bills and payments. By knowing when your bills are due and how much they are, you can avoid late fees and penalties.

It also allows you to see if there are any bills you can negotiate or cut back on to save money.

Thirdly, tracking your expenses can help you save money. When you see how much you're spending on non-essential items, you can make adjustments to your spending habits and put that money towards savings or paying off debt.

How to Track Your Expenses

There are several ways to track your expenses, and the method you choose depends on what works best for you. One of the most popular ways to track expenses is to use a budgeting app or software. There are many free options available, such as Mint or Personal Capital, that allow you to connect your bank accounts and credit cards to track your expenses automatically. These apps also categorize your expenses, so you can see how much you're spending in different areas.

Another way to track your expenses is to use a spreadsheet. You can create your own or use a template, and input your expenses manually. This method requires more effort but allows you to customize your categories and track your expenses more closely.

Alternatively, you can track your expenses with a pen and paper. This method is straightforward but can be time-consuming, especially if you make a lot of transactions.

Whichever method you choose, it's essential to track your expenses regularly. Ideally, you should do this daily, but at the very least, track your expenses weekly. This way, you can see where your money is going in real-time and make adjustments as needed.

What to Track

When tracking your expenses, it's essential to be thorough. Include every expense, no matter how small. Small purchases can add up over time, and it's easy to forget about them if you're not tracking them. Some common expenses to track include:

- Housing expenses (rent or mortgage payments, property taxes, home insurance)
- Utilities (electricity, gas, water, internet, phone)
- Food (groceries, eating out)
- Transportation (gas, public transportation, car repairs)
- Entertainment (movies, concerts, hobbies)
- Personal care (haircuts, toiletries)
- Debt payments (credit cards, loans, medical bills)

- Insurance (health, car, life)
- Savings (retirement, emergency fund)

It's also essential to categorize your expenses. This way, you can see how much you're spending in each category and identify areas where you can cut back. Some common categories include housing, utilities, food, transportation, entertainment, personal care, debt, insurance, and savings.

In addition to tracking your expenses, it's also important to categorize them. You may want to create categories such as groceries, utilities, transportation, housing, entertainment, and so on. This will give you a clear idea of where your money is going each month, and help you identify areas where you may be overspending.

There are many tools available to help you track your expenses, from basic spreadsheets to more sophisticated apps and software programs. Some popular options that we talked about previously include Mint, YNAB (You Need a Budget), Personal Capital, and Quicken.

Regardless of the tool you choose, the key is to be consistent and diligent about tracking your expenses. Make it a habit to record every expense, no matter how small, and review your spending regularly. This will help you stay on top of your finances and make informed decisions about where to cut back and where to allocate more funds.

One technique that can be helpful in tracking your expenses is the envelope system. This involves setting aside cash for different categories of expenses, such as groceries, transportation, and entertainment, and putting each amount in a separate envelope. When you spend money on a particular category, you take the cash from the corresponding envelope. This system can be especially helpful for those who struggle with overspending or impulse buying, as it imposes a physical limit on how much money you can spend in each category.

Another important aspect of tracking your expenses is to be honest with yourself about your spending habits. It can be easy to justify unnecessary purchases or convince yourself that you "deserve" a treat, but ultimately this can lead to financial stress and anxiety. By being honest with yourself about your spending habits, you can identify areas where you need to make changes and take steps to improve your overall financial health.

In conclusion, tracking your expenses is a crucial step in achieving financial freedom. By keeping a close eye on where your money is going each month, you can identify areas where you may be overspending and make informed decisions about where to cut back. Additionally, by categorizing your expenses and using tools like the envelope system, you can stay on top of your finances and make the most of your income. So if you haven't already, start tracking your expenses today – your future self will thank you for it!

Step-by-step guide to getting an overview, budgeting and tracking expenses.

1. Determine your net income: Your net income is the amount of money you earn after taxes and other deductions have been taken out. Gather all possible income sources and calculate what you have left after tax.

2. List all of your expenses: Make a list of all of your monthly expenses, including fixed expenses (like rent/mortgage, car payments, and insurance) and variable expenses (like groceries, gas, and entertainment).

3. Categorize your expenses: Divide your expenses into categories such as housing, transportation, food, and entertainment.

4. Assign a dollar amount to each category: Estimate how much you spend in each category every month. If you're unsure, track your expenses for a month or two to get a more accurate estimate.

5. Set a budget for each category: Based on your estimates, set a monthly budget for each category. For example, the average US household has about 4000$ after taxes, they might allocate $1,200 to housing,

$500 to transportation, $500 to food, and $300 to entertainment.

6. Evaluate your budget: Take a look at your budget and make sure it is realistic and sustainable. If you're not sure, try living within your budget for a month or two to see if it works for you.

7. Make adjustments: If you find that your budget isn't working for you, make adjustments. Look for ways to cut back on expenses in each category. For example, you might try cooking at home more often to save money on food, or finding ways to reduce your transportation expenses.

8. Track your expenses: To stay on top of your budget, track your expenses. This can be done using a spreadsheet or a budgeting app. Make sure to record all of your expenses, even small purchases like a cup of coffee or a snack.

9. Stick to your budget: Once you've set your budget and made adjustments as needed, stick to it. This may require some discipline and sacrifice, but it's important to stay within your budget in order to stay on your track to financial independece.

10. Revisit your budget regularly: Your expenses may change from month to month or year to year, so it's important to revisit your budget regularly. This can

help you identify areas where you may need to make adjustments and ensure that you're on track to reach your financial goals.

# Chapter 2 – Money-Saving Strategies

In this chapter we will talk about micro habits that will help you to save money in your everyday life. Some points seem very basic at first glance but incorporating them into your habits will make a big difference.

Saving money is not always easy, especially when you have bills to pay and unexpected expenses arise. However, by implementing some of the strategies in this chapter, you can reduce your spending and increase your savings. Saving money is not only essential for building an emergency fund and achieving your financial goals, but it can also reduce stress and help you feel more in control of your finances.

In this chapter, we will discuss various money-saving strategies that you can start implementing today. We will cover tips on how to reduce your expenses on groceries, utilities, transportation, and other common expenses. We will also discuss how to take advantage of discounts, promotions, and cashback offers to save money on purchases.

By the end of this chapter, you will have a better understanding of the various money-saving strategies you can use to achieve your financial goals. Whether you want to save money for a down payment on a house, pay off debt, or build an emergency fund, the tips in this chapter will help you get there. So, let's get started!

Plan your purchases in advance.

Planning your purchases in advance can be an effective way to save money and stay on budget. When you plan your purchases, you can take the time to research prices, find deals, and make informed decisions about what you really need. Here are some tips to help you plan your purchases in advance:

1. Make a list: Before you make any purchase, make a list of what you need. This will help you stay focused on your needs and avoid impulse purchases. It's important to be specific in your list, so you know exactly what you're looking for.

2. Research prices: Once you have your list, take the time to research prices. Look for the best deals and compare prices from different retailers. You can use online price comparison tools, browse advertisements, or visit different stores to find the best prices.

3. Set a budget: Based on the prices you've found, set a budget for each item on your list. This will help you stay on track and avoid overspending. If you find that the items on your list are too expensive, consider prioritizing your purchases and buying only the most essential items.

4.  Wait for sales: If possible, wait for sales before making your purchases. Many retailers offer discounts and promotions throughout the year, and you can save a significant amount of money by waiting for these sales. However, make sure you don't wait too long and miss out on the items you need.

5.  Use coupons and promo codes: Another way to save money is by using coupons and promo codes. Many retailers offer discounts and promotions to customers who use these codes. You can find coupons and promo codes online or in advertisements.

6.  Buy in bulk: Buying in bulk can also be a good way to save money. If you know you'll use a certain product regularly, buying it in bulk can help you save money over time. However, make sure you're not buying more than you need, or you could end up wasting money.

7.  Consider alternatives: Finally, consider alternatives to the items on your list. Are there cheaper options that will work just as well? Can you borrow or rent the item instead of buying it? By considering alternatives, you may be able to save money without sacrificing quality or convenience.

Planning your purchases in advance can take some time and effort, but it can be a very effective way to save money and stay on budget. By making a list, researching prices, setting a budget, waiting for sales, using coupons and promo codes, buying in bulk, and considering alternatives, you can make informed decisions about your purchases and avoid overspending.

In the following chapters we will go into even more detail for each of the points mentioned.

Avoid impulse purchases.

Impulse purchases can quickly derail your budget and lead to financial stress. It's easy to get caught up in the moment and buy something you don't really need or can't afford, but with a little discipline and planning, you can avoid impulse purchases and stay on track with your financial goals.

Here are some tips to help you avoid impulse purchases:

1.  Make a list: Before you go shopping, make a list of the items you need to buy. Stick to the list and avoid browsing aisles or sections of the store that don't have items on your list.
2.  Plan your purchases: Plan your purchases ahead of time and do some research to find the best deals. This will help you avoid making last-minute decisions based on emotions.
3.  Avoid temptation: Avoid stores and websites that are known for tempting you with sales and promotions. Instead, focus on retailers that offer fair prices on the items you need.
4.  Delay gratification: When you see something you want, wait a few days before making the purchase. This will give you time to think about whether the item is really necessary and fits within your budget.

5. Use cash: Using cash instead of credit cards can help you avoid impulse purchases. When you have a limited amount of cash on hand, you're more likely to think twice before making a purchase.

6. Shop alone: Shopping with friends or family can be fun, but it can also lead to impulse purchases. If you're trying to stick to a budget, consider shopping alone or with someone who shares your financial goals.

7. Avoid shopping when you're emotional: If you're feeling stressed, anxious, or upset, avoid shopping. Emotions can cloud your judgment and make you more likely to make impulsive purchases.

8. Stick to your budget: Set a budget for each shopping trip and stick to it. If you find something you really want but it's not within your budget, wait until you can afford it or find a cheaper alternative.

9. Remember your financial goals: When you're tempted to make an impulse purchase, think about your financial goals. Do you want to save for a down payment on a house or pay off debt? Remembering your long-term goals can help you stay on track and avoid unnecessary purchases.

10. Find alternatives: If you're tempted to make an impulse purchase, consider finding a cheaper alternative. For example, if you want a new outfit,

look for secondhand clothing or shop at discount stores.

In conclusion, impulse purchases can wreak havoc on your budget and financial goals. But with a little planning, discipline, and self-awareness, you can avoid them and stay on track with your finances. Remember to make a list, plan your purchases, avoid temptation, delay gratification, use cash, shop alone, avoid emotional shopping, stick to your budget, remember your financial goals, and find alternatives. With these tips, you'll be able to make smarter, more intentional purchasing decisions and achieve financial freedom.

Shop around for deals.

Shopping around for deals can be an effective way to save money on your purchases. Whether you're buying groceries, clothing, or electronics, taking the time to compare prices and look for discounts can make a big difference in your overall budget.

The first step in shopping around for deals is to know what you're looking for. Before you start shopping, make a list of the items you need, and decide on your budget for each item. This will help you stay focused and avoid overspending.

Next, do your research. Look for sales, discounts, and promotions at different stores and websites. Check out weekly ads, coupon websites, and social media pages for deals on the items you need. You can also sign up for email newsletters from your favorite retailers to receive notifications about upcoming sales and special offers.

Another way to save money is to compare prices at different stores. Check online and in-store prices, and make note of any price matching policies. Some stores will match or beat competitors' prices, so don't be afraid to ask.

When shopping online, it's important to factor in shipping costs and delivery times. While some websites offer free shipping, others may charge a fee or have a minimum purchase amount. Make sure to read the fine print before making your purchase.

Timing can also play a role in finding the best deals. For example, shopping for seasonal items after the season has ended can result in significant discounts. Additionally, some retailers offer clearance sales at the end of each season to make room for new inventory.

When shopping for big-ticket items, such as electronics or appliances, it's important to do your research beforehand. Read reviews and compare prices to find the best deals. You can also look for refurbished or gently used items, which are often significantly cheaper than new ones.

In addition to traditional retailers, consider checking out local flea markets, thrift stores, and consignment shops. These places can be treasure troves for unique finds and hidden gems. You may be surprised at the quality of items you can find for a fraction of the cost of new ones.

One important thing to keep in mind when shopping around for deals is to avoid impulse purchases. Just because something is on sale doesn't necessarily mean you need it or that it's a good deal for you. Stick to your budget and your list, and only purchase items that you truly need or have been planning to buy.

Finally, make sure to keep track of your purchases and the prices you paid for them. This can help you identify patterns and trends in pricing, as well as determine the best times to shop for certain items. You can use a spreadsheet or budgeting app to help you stay organized.

Shopping around for deals may require some extra time and effort, but the savings can be significant. By doing your research, comparing prices, and avoiding impulse purchases, you can stretch your budget and get the most value for your money.

Buy things on sale.

When it comes to making purchases, saving money is always a good thing. One of the easiest ways to save money is to buy things on sale. Whether it's groceries, clothes, or electronics, buying items on sale can help you stretch your budget further. In this chapter, we'll take a closer look at the benefits of buying things on sale, and offer some tips to help you make the most of your sale shopping.

Benefits of buying things on sale:

1. Save money: The most obvious benefit of buying things on sale is the cost savings. When you buy something on sale, you're paying less than you would if you bought it at full price. These savings can really add up over time, especially if you're buying items that you need regularly, such as groceries.

2. Get more for your money: When you buy something on sale, you're often getting more for your money. For example, you might be able to buy two items for the price of one, or get a larger size for the same price as a smaller one. This can help you stretch your budget further and get more value for your money.

3. Try new things: Sales can be a great opportunity to try new things that you might not have considered

otherwise. For example, if you've been curious about a certain type of food but weren't willing to pay full price for it, a sale can give you the chance to try it without breaking the bank.

Tips for buying things on sale:

1. Plan ahead: One of the keys to successful sale shopping is to plan ahead. Make a list of the items you need and keep an eye out for sales on those items. This can help you avoid impulse purchases and ensure that you're only buying what you need.

2. Do your research: Before you buy something on sale, do your research to make sure that you're really getting a good deal. Check the regular price of the item and compare it to the sale price. You might also want to check other stores to see if they're offering the same item for a lower price.

3. Shop at the right time: Shopping at the right time can help you get the best deals. For example, many stores have sales at the end of each season to clear out their inventory. You might also want to shop on weekdays, when there are fewer shoppers and the stores are less crowded.

4. Use coupons and promo codes: In addition to sales, many stores and online shops offer coupons and

promo codes that can help you save even more money. Before you make a purchase, do a quick search online to see if there are any coupons or promo codes available.

5. Don't buy just because it's on sale: While it can be tempting to buy something just because it's on sale, it's important to remember that you're only saving money if you're buying something you actually need. Before you make a purchase, ask yourself if you really need the item and if you would have bought it at full price.

6. Buy in bulk: Buying in bulk can help you save money in the long run. For example, if you know that you'll be using a certain type of food regularly, buying a larger quantity of it when it's on sale can help you save money over time.

7. Be mindful of quality: When buying things on sale, it's important to be mindful of quality. While you might be able to get a good deal on a certain item, it's not worth it if the item is of poor quality and won't last very long. Make sure that you're getting a good deal on a quality item that will last you for a while.

In conclusion, buying things on sale is a great way to save money and stick to your budget while still being able to purchase the things you need and want. By being mindful of sales cycles, planning ahead, and taking advantage of discounts, you can enjoy significant savings on a wide range of products.

However, it's important to remember that not all sales are created equal. Just because something is on sale doesn't necessarily mean it's a good deal, and it's important to do your research and compare prices before making a purchase.

Ultimately, the key to successful bargain shopping is finding a balance between sticking to your budget and getting the most value for your money. By following the tips and strategies outlined in this chapter, you can become a savvy shopper and make the most of your hard-earned money. Happy shopping!

## Buy in bulk.

In addition to buying things on sale, its also important to compare prices for the amount of the product you get. Another easy way to save money on your groceries is therefore to buy in bulk. Buying in bulk means purchasing larger quantities of food items at once, usually at a lower price per unit. This is a great way to save money on items that you use regularly, such as rice, pasta, cereal, and other non-perishable goods.

Here are some tips on how to buy in bulk and save money on your groceries:

1. Identify the items you use frequently: Before you start buying in bulk, make a list of the items that you use regularly. This could include pantry staples like rice, pasta, and canned goods, as well as cleaning supplies and toiletries. By focusing on the items that you use most often, you'll ensure that you're getting the most value for your money.

2. Check the unit price: Buying in bulk can be a great way to save money, but it's important to make sure you're actually getting a good deal. Check the unit price of the items you're considering purchasing, which is usually listed on the shelf tag or label. This

will help you compare the price per unit of different sizes and brands to see which one offers the best value.

3. Shop at wholesale clubs: Wholesale clubs like Costco and Sam's Club are great places to buy in bulk. They offer a wide range of products at lower prices than you'd find at traditional grocery stores. However, keep in mind that you'll need to pay an annual membership fee to shop at these stores, so make sure the savings you'll get on your purchases will offset the cost of the membership.

4. Use coupons: Many retailers offer coupons for bulk purchases, which can help you save even more money. Look for coupons in your local newspaper or online, and make sure to read the fine print to see if there are any restrictions on the items you can purchase.

5. Store food properly: When buying in bulk, it's important to store your food properly to prevent spoilage and waste. Make sure to use airtight containers to store dry goods, and freeze meat and other perishable items that you won't use right away. This will help you make the most of your bulk purchases and save money in the long run.

6. Plan your meals: Buying in bulk can be a great way to save money, but it's important to plan your meals

carefully to avoid waste. Before you head to the store, make a meal plan for the week based on the items you've purchased in bulk. This will help you use up your supplies before they expire, and reduce the risk of food waste.

7. Share with friends or family: If you don't think you'll be able to use all of the items you've purchased in bulk, consider sharing with friends or family members. This is a great way to split the cost of bulk purchases and reduce waste.

Buying in bulk is a great way to save money on your groceries, but it's important to be mindful of your purchases. By focusing on the items you use most often, checking the unit price, shopping at wholesale clubs, using coupons, storing food properly, planning your meals, and sharing with others, you can make the most of your bulk purchases and save money in the long run.

A short example:

Let's say you're at the grocery store and you need to buy cereal. You see two different brands of cereal, one in a smaller box for $3.99 and another in a larger box for $5.99. At first glance, you might think that the smaller box is the better deal since it costs less. However, by checking the unit price, you can determine which option is actually more cost-effective.

The unit price is the price per unit of measurement, such as per ounce or per pound. To find the unit price of each cereal option, you'll need to look at the label on each box. Let's say the smaller box contains 10 ounces of cereal and the larger box contains 20 ounces of cereal.

To calculate the unit price of the smaller box, divide the price by the number of ounces:

$3.99 / 10 ounces = $0.399 per ounce

To calculate the unit price of the larger box, divide the price by the number of ounces:

$5.99 / 20 ounces = $0.2995 per ounce

In this case, the larger box is actually the better deal because it has a lower unit price per ounce. Even though the larger box costs more upfront, you'll save money in the long run by buying in bulk and getting a lower unit price.

By checking the unit price, you can make informed purchasing decisions and avoid overpaying for products. This strategy is particularly useful for items that you buy frequently, such as groceries and household supplies. Over time, the savings from buying at a lower unit price can add up significantly.

Cook at home instead of eating out.

Cooking at home instead of eating out is one of the most effective ways to save money and improve your financial health. Eating out can quickly add up, and the cost of a single meal at a restaurant can be equivalent to what you might spend on groceries for an entire week. By cooking at home, you not only save money, but you also have greater control over the quality and nutrition of your meals.

Here are some tips for cooking at home to save money:

1. Plan your meals in advance: Planning your meals ahead of time allows you to buy only the ingredients you need and avoid wasting money on unnecessary items. You can plan your meals for the week on a Sunday and make a grocery list accordingly.

2. Buy ingredients in bulk: Buying ingredients in bulk can be a great way to save money. Consider buying staples like rice, beans, and pasta in larger quantities to save money over time.

3. Use leftovers: Instead of throwing away leftover food, use it to make another meal. For example, leftover vegetables can be turned into a stir-fry or soup, and leftover chicken can be used in a salad or sandwich.

4. Cook in batches: Cooking in batches can save time and money. You can cook a large batch of soup, stew, or chili and freeze portions for later use. This way, you can have a quick and healthy meal ready when you don't have the time or energy to cook from scratch.

5. Use coupons and sales: Look for sales and coupons at your local grocery store. You can also sign up for store loyalty programs that offer discounts and rewards. This can help you save money on groceries and make cooking at home more affordable.

6. Avoid pre-packaged and processed foods: Pre-packaged and processed foods are often more expensive and less healthy than fresh, whole foods. Try to avoid pre-packaged meals, snacks, and convenience foods and focus on making meals from scratch.

7. Cook with seasonal ingredients: Seasonal ingredients are often less expensive and more flavorful than out-of-season produce. Look for seasonal produce at your local farmers' market or grocery store and plan your meals around these ingredients.

8. Invest in basic kitchen tools: Investing in basic kitchen tools like a good knife, cutting board, and pots and pans can make cooking at home easier and more enjoyable. You don't need to spend a lot of money,

but having a few quality tools can make a big difference.

Cooking at home can be a fun and rewarding experience. Not only does it save you money, but it also allows you to have greater control over what you eat and the quality of your meals. With a little planning and some basic kitchen skills, you can make delicious and healthy meals at home without breaking the bank.

In addition to saving money, cooking at home can also have health benefits. Eating out often means consuming larger portions and more calories, salt, and sugar than you might consume at home. By cooking at home, you can control the ingredients and portion sizes, making it easier to eat healthier and maintain a healthy weight.

In conclusion, cooking at home instead of eating out is a simple but effective way to save money and improve your financial health. By planning your meals, buying ingredients in bulk, using leftovers, cooking in batches, using coupons and sales, avoiding pre-packaged and processed foods, cooking with seasonal ingredients, and investing in basic kitchen tools, you can make delicious and healthy meals at home without breaking the bank. So, next time you're tempted to eat out, consider cooking at home instead – your wallet and your health will thank you.

Bring your lunch to work.

This is an addition to the prior chapter, because one of the biggest expenses that many people have is eating out for lunch during the workday. It's easy to fall into the habit of grabbing a quick sandwich or salad from a nearby deli or fast-food chain, but those daily expenses can add up quickly. One of the simplest and most effective ways to save money on food expenses is to bring your lunch to work instead of eating out.

There are a variety of reasons why bringing your lunch to work can be beneficial. For one, it's often cheaper to make your own meals at home than it is to buy lunch from a restaurant or cafe every day. When you make your own lunch, you have control over the ingredients and portion sizes, which can also be healthier than eating out.

Another benefit of bringing your lunch to work is that it can be a time-saver. Instead of spending time waiting in line at a restaurant or trying to decide where to eat, you can simply grab your lunch from the fridge and get back to work. This can be especially helpful if you have a busy schedule or if you're trying to get more done during the workday.

To get started with bringing your lunch to work, you'll need to do a bit of planning and preparation. One of the first things you should do is figure out what kinds of foods you enjoy and are easy to prepare. This might involve trying out some new recipes or simply making larger portions of meals you already enjoy and can easily pack for lunch.

Another important step is to make sure you have the right containers and tools for packing your lunch. You might want to invest in some reusable containers, such as Tupperware or glass jars, that are sturdy and can keep your food fresh. You'll also need a lunch bag or cooler to keep your food at the right temperature.

When you're packing your lunch, it's important to think about both variety and nutrition. Aim to include a mix of different food groups, such as protein, vegetables, and whole grains. You might also want to consider packing some healthy snacks, such as fruit or nuts, to help keep you satisfied throughout the day.

One of the keys to successfully bringing your lunch to work is to make it as convenient and enjoyable as possible. This might mean setting aside some time each evening or morning to pack your lunch, or even prepping some ingredients or meals over the weekend. You might also want to consider making your lunch more enjoyable by packing it with some of your favorite foods or flavors.

Of course, there may be times when you simply can't bring your lunch to work, such as when you have an important meeting or event that involves food. In those cases, it's still possible to save money by looking for ways to eat out for less. This might involve seeking out lunch specials or discounts, or simply choosing more affordable options on the menu.

Bringing your lunch to work can be a small but effective way to save money and improve your overall health and wellbeing. By taking the time to plan and prepare your meals, you can enjoy a variety of delicious and healthy foods while also saving money and time during the workday. Whether you're just starting out or are already an experienced meal prepper, there are always new ideas and strategies to try to make your lunchtime routine even more enjoyable and rewarding.

Avoid buying bottled water.

Drinking water is essential for our health, and staying hydrated throughout the day is crucial. However, buying bottled water can be expensive and wasteful. The cost of bottled water can add up over time, especially if you are a frequent buyer. In addition to being a financial burden, buying bottled water can also harm the environment. Plastic water bottles are not biodegradable, and they contribute to the growing problem of plastic pollution in our oceans and landfills.

To save money and help the environment, you can avoid buying bottled water altogether. Instead, consider investing in a reusable water bottle and filling it up with tap water. Here are some ways in which avoiding bottled water can save you money:

1. Save money on the cost of bottled water: Bottled water can be expensive, especially if you are buying it regularly. A typical bottle of water can cost anywhere from $1 to $2, and the cost can quickly add up over time. For example, if you buy a $1 bottle of water every day for a month, you would end up spending $30. How would this look annually? According to the Beverage Marketing Corporation, the average cost of a

16.9-ounce bottle of water is $1.29. If you drink one bottle of water a day, that's over $470 per year. In contrast, tap water costs less than a penny per gallon.

2. Reduce your grocery bill: If you are someone who buys bottled water in bulk, avoiding bottled water can save you money on your grocery bill. Buying a case of bottled water can cost anywhere from $5 to $10, depending on the brand and quantity. However, if you invest in a reusable water bottle, you can save money in the long run.

3. Save money when eating out: If you are someone who frequently eats out, you may notice that restaurants charge a premium for bottled water. By bringing your reusable water bottle with you, you can save money and reduce your environmental impact.

4. Save money on transportation costs: If you are someone who buys bottled water on the go, you may be spending money on transportation costs to get to the store. By avoiding bottled water, you can save money on transportation costs, as well as reduce your carbon footprint.

In addition to saving money, avoiding bottled water can also benefit the environment. Here are some ways in which avoiding bottled water can be environmentally friendly:

1. Reduce plastic waste: Plastic water bottles are not biodegradable and can take hundreds of years to decompose. By using a reusable water bottle, you can reduce your contribution to plastic waste.

2. Save energy: The production and transportation of bottled water require a significant amount of energy. By avoiding bottled water, you can reduce the demand for energy, which can help reduce greenhouse gas emissions.

3. Protect natural resources: Bottled water companies often extract water from natural sources, such as springs and aquifers. By using tap water, you can help protect these natural resources.

4. Reduce pollution: The production, transportation, and disposal of plastic water bottles can contribute to air and water pollution. By avoiding bottled water, you can help reduce pollution and protect the environment.

In conclusion, avoiding bottled water can be a simple and effective way to save money and help the environment. By investing in a reusable water bottle and filling it up with tap water, you can reduce your carbon footprint and contribute to a more sustainable future.

Use cash instead of credit/debit cards.

In today's world, it's easier than ever to swipe a credit card for every purchase we make. While it may be convenient, it can also lead to overspending and debt. That's why using cash instead of credit cards can be a smart financial move. In this chapter, we'll discuss the benefits of using cash, how to make the transition from credit cards to cash, and tips for making it work for you.

One of the biggest advantages of using cash is that it's a physical representation of the money you have. When you use cash, you're forced to stick to a budget because once the cash is gone, it's gone. With credit cards, it's easy to overspend and lose track of how much you've actually spent. This can lead to carrying a balance and paying high interest rates.

Using cash can also help you save money in the long run. When you pay with cash, you're more likely to think twice about your purchases and make more mindful choices. You may even find yourself negotiating prices and seeking out deals to make the most of your money. Plus, since you're not accruing interest on purchases, you'll have more money to put towards savings or paying off debt.

Making the switch from credit cards to cash may seem daunting at first, but it's important to remember that it's a process. Start by setting a budget for yourself and withdrawing cash at the beginning of the week or month. Then, make sure to only use the cash for the purchases within your budget. You may find it helpful to leave your credit cards at home or even freeze them in a block of ice to avoid temptation.

Another key to successfully using cash is to track your spending. Keep a log of each purchase you make, including the date, amount, and category of the purchase. This will help you stay accountable to your budget and identify areas where you may need to cut back.

If you're used to using credit cards for rewards or cash back, there are still ways to make the most of your spending while using cash. Consider using cash back apps or rewards programs that allow you to earn points for purchases made with cash. You can also look for cash-only discounts or coupons to maximize your savings.

Using cash instead of credit cards does require a bit more planning and effort, but it can be a valuable tool for managing your finances. Here are some additional tips for making the most of your cash:

1. Make a grocery list before heading to the store and only bring the cash you need to make those purchases. This will help you avoid impulse buys and stay within your budget.

2. When shopping for big-ticket items, research prices beforehand to make sure you're getting the best deal. Then, withdraw the exact amount of cash you need for the purchase.

3. If you have a hard time sticking to your budget, consider using an envelope system. Label envelopes with different categories (such as groceries, entertainment, and gas) and allocate a certain amount of cash to each envelope. Once the cash in the envelope is gone, you can't spend any more in that category.

4. Take advantage of free activities and events in your community, rather than spending money on entertainment. This could include visiting a park, attending a free concert, or trying out a new hiking trail.

In conclusion, using cash instead of credit cards can be a smart financial move. It can help you stick to a budget, save money, and make more mindful purchases. While it may take some effort and planning to make the switch, the benefits can be significant. So next time you're considering swiping that credit card, think twice and consider the value of using cash.

Avoid buying things you don't need.

It can be tempting to make impulse purchases, but buying things you don't need can quickly add up and become a drain on your finances. Learning to differentiate between wants and needs is crucial to maintaining a healthy budget.

To start, consider the difference between a want and a need. A need is something that is essential to your daily life, such as food, shelter, and clothing. A want, on the other hand, is something that you desire but is not necessary for survival. For example, a new pair of shoes may be a want, while a reliable pair of shoes for work would be a need.

When you are considering making a purchase, take a moment to evaluate whether it is a want or a need. Ask yourself questions like, "Can I live without this item?" or "Is this something I will use on a regular basis?" If the answer is no, it may be best to avoid making the purchase.

Another way to avoid buying things you don't need is to make a list before you go shopping. Creating a list can help you stay focused on the items you actually need, rather than getting distracted by impulse buys. Stick to your list and avoid browsing the aisles, as this can lead to buying items you don't need.

It's also essential to be aware of the marketing tactics that retailers use to entice you to buy things you don't need. Retailers often use sales and discounts to create a sense of urgency and encourage impulse purchases. Remember that just because an item is on sale doesn't necessarily mean it's a good deal or something you need. Stick to your list and budget to avoid getting lured into making unnecessary purchases.

When you do find yourself tempted to make an impulse purchase, try implementing the 24-hour rule. This means waiting 24 hours before making a purchase to give yourself time to consider whether you really need the item. More often than not, you may find that the impulse to buy has passed, and you can save yourself from making an unnecessary purchase.

Another useful tip is to avoid shopping when you are feeling emotional or stressed. Studies have shown that when we are feeling down or stressed, we are more likely to make impulse purchases. Take a break, go for a walk, or engage in an activity you enjoy before going shopping. This can help clear your mind and reduce the chances of making purchases you don't need.

Finally, consider the long-term cost of buying things you don't need. While it may seem like a small purchase at the time, these items can add up over time and impact your ability to save and invest for the future. By avoiding unnecessary purchases and focusing on your needs, you can free up more money to put towards your financial goals.

In conclusion, avoiding buying things you don't need is essential to maintaining a healthy budget and achieving financial freedom. By differentiating between wants and needs, creating a list before shopping, being aware of marketing tactics, implementing the 24-hour rule, avoiding emotional shopping, and considering the long-term cost, you can make informed decisions about your purchases and keep your finances on track. Remember that every purchase you make has an impact on your financial future, so take the time to consider whether you really need the item before making the purchase.

Don't buy things just because they are on sale.

"Wait a minute. You just told me to buy things when they are on sale and now I shouldn't?"

Exactly, there is a huge difference between buying thigs (you need) on sale and buying things (you might not necessarily need) <u>JUST BECAUSE</u> they are on sale. Buying things just because they are on sale can be a tempting prospect. After all, who doesn't like to save money? However, this can often lead to unnecessary purchases that end up costing you more in the long run. In this chapter, we will explore why it's important to resist the urge to buy things just because they are on sale and how to avoid this common shopping trap.

One of the biggest dangers of buying things just because they are on sale is that it can lead to impulse purchases. When we see something at a discounted price, our brains can trick us into thinking that we are getting a great deal, even if we don't really need the item. This can be especially true for items that we have been eyeing for a while, but couldn't justify the cost. When we see these items on sale, we can convince ourselves that it's the perfect time to buy, even if we don't really need them.

Another issue with buying things just because they are on sale is that it can lead to clutter and wastefulness. When we accumulate items that we don't really need or use, they can take up valuable space in our homes and lives. This can lead to clutter and disorganization, making it harder to find and use the things that we actually need. Additionally, when we buy things that we don't really need, they can end up going to waste, either because we never end up using them, or because they go bad or expire before we get a chance to use them.

To avoid falling into the trap of buying things just because they are on sale, it's important to approach shopping with a plan. Start by making a list of the things that you actually need or have been meaning to buy. This could include items like groceries, household supplies, or clothing. Once you have a list, do some research to find the best deals and prices. This could involve checking store flyers, browsing online retailers, or even contacting local businesses to see if they have any promotions or discounts.

When you do come across a sale, take a moment to ask yourself if the item is something that you actually need or want. Consider whether you would buy the item if it weren't on sale, and whether you have the money to pay for it without going over your budget. If you do decide to buy the item, make sure that you are getting a good deal by checking the original price and the sale price, as well as any additional discounts or promotions that may be available.

Another helpful tip for avoiding impulse purchases is to give yourself a cooling off period. If you see something on sale that you think you want, but aren't sure if you actually need, take a step back and wait a day or two before making the purchase. This can give you time to think more clearly about whether the item is something that you really want or need, or whether you were just caught up in the excitement of the sale.

It's also important to be mindful of your shopping habits and to avoid situations that may trigger impulsive buying. For example, if you know that you are susceptible to impulse purchases when shopping with friends, consider going shopping alone instead. If you find that you are more likely to buy things on sale when you are feeling stressed or anxious, try finding other ways to manage your emotions, such as through exercise or meditation.

In summary, buying things just because they are on sale can be a dangerous shopping trap that leads to impulse purchases, clutter, and wastefulness. To avoid falling into this trap, it's important to approach shopping with a plan and to be mindful of your shopping habits. Make a list of the things that you actually need or have been meaning to buy, research the best deals and prices, and give yourself a cooling off period before making any impulsive purchases. As you see, we are revisiting some topics that we talked about before. This is because many of these go hand in hand and together, they will have a great impact if you make habits out of them.

Don't buy things just because they are (or seem) cheap.

When it comes to shopping, many people are drawn to items that are priced low, even if they don't actually need them. While it may seem like a good deal in the moment, buying things just because they are cheap can actually end up costing you more in the long run. In this chapter, we will explore the reasons why it's important to resist the urge to buy things just because they are cheap.

One of the main problems with buying things just because they are cheap is that it can lead to clutter in your home. When you buy things that you don't need, you are essentially adding to the number of items you own, which can quickly pile up and take up valuable space in your home. Not only does this create a physical burden, but it can also lead to mental clutter as well. When your living space is cluttered, it can be difficult to focus and feel relaxed in your own home.

Another issue with buying things just because they are cheap is that it can lead to overspending. Just because something is inexpensive doesn't mean that it fits into your budget or that you can afford it. If you consistently buy items that you don't need just because they are priced low, you may end up spending more than you intended and potentially putting yourself in a financially precarious situation.

In addition to clutter and overspending, buying things just because they are cheap can also contribute to a culture of waste. When you buy items that you don't need or won't use, they often end up being thrown away or donated, which can be a waste of resources and contribute to environmental problems. By being mindful of your purchasing habits and only buying things that you truly need, you can help reduce waste and be more environmentally responsible.

So how can you avoid buying things just because they are cheap? The first step is to be mindful of your purchasing habits. Before making a purchase, ask yourself if the item is something that you actually need or if it's just something that caught your eye because of its low price. If it's the latter, take a step back and reconsider whether or not it's worth spending money on.

Another helpful tip is to avoid impulse purchases. When you see something that's priced low, it can be tempting to buy it on the spot without really thinking it through. Instead, make a habit of taking a step back and giving yourself some time to think about whether or not you really need the item. This can help you avoid making impulsive purchases and buying things just because they are cheap.

It can also be helpful to set a budget for yourself and stick to it. This will help you avoid overspending and make more mindful purchasing decisions. When you have a budget in place, you are less likely to be swayed by low prices or impulse purchases, and you can focus on buying only the things that you truly need.

Finally, consider the long-term cost of your purchases. While something may be cheap in the moment, it may end up costing you more in the long run if it's not something that you truly need or if it's not made to last. When making purchasing decisions, think about the long-term value of the item and whether or not it's worth spending money on.

In conclusion, buying things just because they are cheap may seem like a good idea in the moment, but it can lead to clutter, overspending, waste, and environmental problems. By being mindful of your purchasing habits, avoiding impulse purchases, setting a budget, and considering the long-term value of your purchases, you can avoid falling into the trap of buying things just because they are cheap. Remember, it's not about the price tag - it's about whether or not the item is something that you truly need and will bring value to your life.

Don't buy things just because they are popular.

The world we live in is often driven by trends and fads, and it's easy to get swept up in the hype. Popular products and brands are constantly being advertised to us, and we are bombarded with messages telling us what we should buy and why. However, just because something is popular doesn't mean that it's the right choice for you or your finances. In fact, succumbing to the pressure of buying things just because they are popular can be a major drain on your bank account. In this chapter, we will explore the dangers of buying things simply because they are popular and provide tips for making more informed purchasing decisions.

The Danger of Popularity

One of the biggest dangers of buying things just because they are popular is that they are often more expensive. When a product is in high demand, manufacturers and retailers know that they can charge a premium for it. This is especially true for luxury items like designer clothes, watches, and cars, which are often seen as status symbols. By buying these items, you may be paying more for the brand name or the status associated with owning them, rather than the actual value of the product.

Another danger of buying things just because they are popular is that they may not actually meet your needs. Popular products are often marketed to a wide audience, but that doesn't mean that they are the right choice for everyone. For example, just because a certain brand of running shoes is popular doesn't mean that they will be the best fit for your feet. By choosing products based on popularity rather than your own needs, you may end up wasting money on things that you don't actually use or enjoy.

Making Informed Purchasing Decisions

So, how can you avoid falling into the trap of buying things just because they are popular? The key is to make informed purchasing decisions based on your own needs and values. Here are some tips to help you make more mindful choices:

1. Identify your values: Before making a purchase, take some time to think about your values and what is important to you. Are you more concerned with quality or price? Do you prioritize sustainability or convenience? By understanding your own values, you can make purchasing decisions that align with your priorities.

2. Do your research: Before buying a product, do some research to find out if it is actually worth the cost.

Read reviews from other customers and compare prices across different retailers. This will help you make a more informed decision and ensure that you are getting the best value for your money.

3. Consider the long-term costs: When making a purchasing decision, it's important to consider the long-term costs as well as the upfront price. For example, a cheaper product may seem like a better deal initially, but if it requires frequent repairs or replacement, it may end up costing you more in the long run. On the other hand, a higher-priced product may be more durable and last longer, ultimately saving you money over time.

4. Don't be swayed by marketing: Marketing is designed to persuade you to buy a particular product, even if it doesn't actually meet your needs. Be aware of marketing tactics like celebrity endorsements and limited-time offers, and don't let them influence your purchasing decisions.

5. Think about the impact of your purchase: Consider the impact that your purchasing decisions have on the environment and society. Are you supporting companies that engage in unethical practices or contribute to environmental harm? By making more

mindful choices, you can support companies that align with your values and contribute to positive change.

Buying things just because they are popular is a dangerous trap that can lead to overspending and wasted money. By making more informed purchasing decisions based on your own needs and values, you can avoid falling for marketing hype and ensure that you spend you money where it matters more.

Avoid ads.

In today's society, advertisements are all around us, and it can be challenging to avoid them. Companies use advertising to persuade us to buy their products, and it's often difficult to resist their messages. However, avoiding ads can help us save money and make more mindful purchases. In this chapter, we'll explore some ways to avoid ads and their impact on our finances.

The first step to avoiding ads is to become aware of them. Advertisements are everywhere, from billboards to social media platforms. They are designed to grab our attention and entice us to buy something. By being aware of ads, we can start to notice when we're being targeted and take steps to avoid them.

One way to avoid ads is to limit our exposure to them. For example, we can unsubscribe from marketing emails and block ads on our web browsers. We can also limit our time on social media, which is often filled with targeted ads. By reducing our exposure to ads, we can minimize their impact on our purchasing decisions.

Another way to avoid ads is to be mindful of the media we consume. Many forms of media, such as TV shows, movies, and video games, contain product placements and advertisements. By being mindful of these ads, we can make more informed purchasing decisions. For example, if we notice a product placement in a TV show, we can take a moment to consider whether we really need that product or if it's just being marketed to us.

We can also avoid ads by doing research before making a purchase. Instead of relying on ads to inform our purchasing decisions, we can seek out information from other sources. For example, we can read product reviews, ask friends for recommendations, and compare prices at different stores. By doing research, we can make more informed decisions and avoid falling for marketing tactics.

It's also important to be aware of the emotional impact of ads. Advertisements often create a sense of urgency, making us feel like we need to buy something right away. They also tap into our emotions, such as fear, desire, and social status. By being aware of these emotional triggers, we can resist the urge to make impulse purchases based on ads.

In addition, it's important to recognize that not all ads are created equal. Some ads are informative and can help us discover new products that are genuinely useful or necessary. However, other ads are purely designed to manipulate us into buying something we don't need or want. By learning to distinguish between these two types of ads, we can make more mindful purchasing decisions.

Finally, it's important to remember that we are in control of our purchasing decisions. While ads can be persuasive, we ultimately have the power to choose whether or not to buy something. By being mindful of our purchasing habits and avoiding ads, we can make more intentional decisions that align with our values and financial goals.

In conclusion, avoiding ads can be a powerful tool for managing our finances. By becoming aware of ads, limiting our exposure to them, doing research, and being mindful of our emotions, we can resist the urge to make impulsive purchases and make more intentional decisions. It's important to remember that we are in control of our purchasing decisions and that ads don't have to dictate our spending habits.

Research before making any major purchases.

When it comes to making major purchases, it's easy to get caught up in the excitement of the moment and make impulsive decisions. However, taking the time to research before making any significant purchase can save you a lot of money in the long run. In this chapter, we'll discuss why it's essential to do your research and some strategies for doing so effectively.

Why Is Research Important Before Making Major Purchases?

There are many reasons why it's crucial to do your research before making any significant purchase, including:

1. To Get the Best Deal: With a little bit of research, you can often find the same product or service at a much lower price. This can save you a lot of money in the long run.

2. To Avoid Buyer's Remorse: Making an impulse purchase can lead to buyer's remorse when you realize that you didn't get the best deal or the product doesn't meet your needs. By doing your research, you can be confident in your purchase and avoid regret.

3. To Make an Informed Decision: Researching before making a significant purchase allows you to make an informed decision based on the features, benefits, and drawbacks of the product or service.

4. To Avoid Scams and Fraud: Unfortunately, there are many scams and fraudulent products and services out there. By doing your research, you can avoid falling prey to these scams and protect your finances.

Strategies for Researching Major Purchases

Now that we've covered why it's crucial to research before making significant purchases let's discuss some strategies for doing so effectively:

1.  Read Reviews: One of the best ways to research a product or service is to read reviews from other customers. This can help you get an idea of the quality of the product, customer service, and any potential issues you may encounter.

2.  Compare Prices: Before making a purchase, be sure to compare prices from different retailers or providers. This can help you find the best deal and save you money.

3.  Research Alternatives: Before committing to a particular product or service, be sure to research alternatives. There may be a more affordable or better-suited option out there that you haven't considered.

4.  Ask for Recommendations: Reach out to friends, family, or colleagues who may have experience with the product or service you're considering. They may be able to offer valuable insights or recommendations.

5.  Look for Sales or Promotions: Keep an eye out for sales or promotions that may be available for the

product or service you're considering. This can help you save money and get a better deal.

6. Check the Return Policy: Before making a purchase, be sure to check the return policy. This can help you avoid any issues if the product doesn't meet your needs.

7. Consider Long-Term Costs: When making a significant purchase, it's essential to consider the long-term costs associated with it. This may include maintenance, repairs, or ongoing expenses that can add up over time.

8. Research the Provider: If you're considering a service provider, be sure to research the company before committing. This can help you avoid scams or fraudulent providers and ensure you're working with a reputable company.

Conclusion

Researching before making a significant purchase can save you money, help you make an informed decision, and protect your finances. By following the strategies outlined in this chapter, you can effectively research products and services, find the best deals, and avoid scams or fraudulent providers. Remember, taking the time to research before making a significant purchase is a crucial step in achieving financial success.

## Cut down on subscriptions.

According to a recent survey by Waterstone Group, the average American spends approximately $237 per month on subscription services. This includes everything from streaming services like Netflix and Hulu to monthly subscription boxes for beauty products, snacks, and more. Breaking it down further, the survey found that the average American subscribes to three streaming services, spending an average of $47 per month on these services alone.

In today's world, it's easier than ever to subscribe to services that offer everything from streaming movies and music to news and magazines. While these services can be convenient and enjoyable, they can also quickly add up and become a significant monthly expense. Cutting down on subscriptions is an effective way to save money and keep your budget under control.

The first step to cutting down on subscriptions is to take an inventory of what you currently subscribe to. Make a list of all the services you pay for each month, including things like Netflix, Hulu, Spotify, gym memberships, and meal delivery services. Then, evaluate each subscription and ask yourself whether or not you really need it.

For example, if you have a gym membership but rarely use it, it may be time to cancel it and find alternative ways to exercise, such as running or hiking outdoors. If you have several streaming services, consider canceling some of them and sticking to just one or two. You may also be able to find free alternatives to some of the services you pay for, such as using a library card to borrow ebooks instead of paying for a Kindle Unlimited subscription.

Another way to cut down on subscriptions is to look for ways to bundle services together. For example, if you subscribe to multiple news and magazine services, you may be able to find a bundle deal that offers access to all of them for a lower price. Similarly, some cable and internet providers offer bundle packages that can save you money on both services.

If you're still having trouble cutting down on subscriptions, consider using a budgeting app that can help you track your spending and identify areas where you can save money. Some budgeting apps even have a feature that specifically tracks your subscriptions and alerts you if you're spending too much on them.

It's also important to be mindful of free trial periods. Many subscription services offer a free trial period that automatically converts to a paid subscription if you don't cancel it in time.

Make sure to set reminders to cancel free trials before they convert to a paid subscription.

When it comes to cutting down on subscriptions, it's important to remember that you don't have to completely eliminate everything you enjoy. Instead, focus on finding a balance between what you need and what you can afford. Consider finding alternative ways to access the same content or services without paying for subscriptions.

In summary, cutting down on subscriptions is a simple and effective way to save money and keep your budget under control. Evaluate each subscription you currently pay for and ask yourself whether or not you really need it. Look for ways to bundle services together, find free alternatives, and use budgeting apps to track your spending. Remember that finding a balance between what you need and what you can afford is key to maintaining a healthy budget.

Cancel unnecessary memberships.

Membership and subscription services are prevalent in modern society. People join these programs for various reasons, including entertainment, fitness, or networking opportunities. However, it is easy to fall into the trap of subscribing to too many memberships and not utilizing them, leading to unnecessary expenses. Canceling unnecessary memberships can save you money and free up your time for other activities. In this chapter, we will explore how to identify and cancel unnecessary memberships.

The first step in canceling unnecessary memberships is to identify which ones you have. This can be a challenging task because it's easy to forget about subscriptions that automatically renew. Start by reviewing your credit card and bank statements to identify recurring charges. You can also check your email for subscription receipts or search through your online accounts for any active memberships.

Once you have identified your memberships, you need to evaluate them to determine their value. Consider how often you use the membership, how much it costs, and whether you can find alternative ways to meet the same needs. For example, if you have a gym membership that you haven't used in months, consider canceling it and finding ways to exercise at home or in your community. Similarly, if you have a streaming service that you only use occasionally, consider canceling it and renting movies or going to the cinema instead.

Another factor to consider when evaluating your memberships is whether they align with your current goals and priorities. For example, if you have a membership to a networking group that no longer aligns with your career aspirations, consider canceling it and finding other ways to network that are more relevant to your current goals.

After evaluating your memberships, you can begin the process of canceling them. Some memberships may require you to cancel in writing, while others may have an online cancellation option. Be sure to read the cancellation policy carefully to avoid any hidden fees or charges. It's also a good idea to keep a record of your cancellation, such as a confirmation email or a copy of a letter you send.

It's important to note that canceling memberships may not be an immediate process. Some memberships require a notice period, which means you may have to continue paying for them for a month or two after canceling. Be sure to factor this into your budgeting and planning.

Canceling unnecessary memberships may seem like a small step, but it can have a significant impact on your finances. Consider the following example: suppose you have five memberships that cost you $20 each per month. By canceling three of them, you will save $60 per month or $720 per year. This money can be redirected toward your savings, debt repayment, or other financial goals.

In addition to saving money, canceling unnecessary memberships can also free up your time and mental energy. When you're not bogged down by a long list of memberships, you have more time to focus on activities that bring you joy and fulfillment. You may find that canceling a few memberships allows you to take up a new hobby, spend more time with loved ones, or pursue a passion project.

It's worth noting that some memberships may be worth keeping even if you don't use them frequently. For example, if you have a subscription to a magazine that you enjoy reading occasionally, it may be worth the cost. However, it's important to be honest with yourself about whether the membership is truly adding value to your life.

Finally, it's essential to be mindful of the temptation to sign up for new memberships in the future. We often sign up for memberships impulsively, without considering whether they are truly necessary or aligned with our goals. Before signing up for a new membership, take the time to evaluate whether it is worth the cost and whether you have the time and energy to use it effectively.

Cancel unnecessary services.

I decided to add this chapter as it differs slightly to the previous two chapters. There are memberships, subscriptions but also services that fall into that category and I feel that we need to talk about these in this specific chapter.

We are constantly inundated with various services that we can sign up for - streaming services, cloud storage, software subscriptions, and more. While these services may seem necessary or convenient at the time of sign-up, they can quickly add up and eat away at your monthly budget. Canceling unnecessary services is one of the easiest ways to reduce your expenses and save money.

The first step in canceling unnecessary services is to evaluate each service you are currently subscribed to. Ask yourself: do I use this service on a regular basis? Does it provide enough value to justify the cost? Is there a cheaper alternative available? By answering these questions, you can determine which services are essential and which ones can be cut.

For example, you may have signed up for a monthly cloud storage subscription that you only use a few times a year. In this case, it would make sense to cancel the subscription and switch to a pay-per-use option or a lower storage plan that better fits your needs. Another example could be a subscription to a news or magazine service that you no longer have time to read. In this case, canceling the subscription would be a smart move as it is no longer providing value.

Once you have identified the services you want to cancel, the next step is to review the cancellation process for each service. Some services may have a simple cancellation process that can be completed online, while others may require a phone call or written notice. It is important to review the terms and conditions of each service to ensure that you are not locked into a contract or will be charged any cancellation fees.

It is important to note that canceling services may not always be a straightforward process. Some companies may try to entice you to stay by offering discounts or free trials, while others may make it difficult to cancel. In these situations, it is important to stand your ground and be firm in your decision to cancel.

Canceling unnecessary services is not just about saving money - it can also help simplify your life. By reducing the number of services you subscribe to, you can cut down on the clutter and focus on the services that truly add value to your life. Additionally, canceling unnecessary services can help reduce stress by reducing the number of bills and payments you need to keep track of.

One of the most common unnecessary services that people subscribe to is a gym membership. While gym memberships can be great for your health and fitness, many people find themselves paying for a membership they never use. If you are one of these people, consider canceling your gym membership and finding alternative ways to stay active. You can exercise outdoors, join a sports team or fitness group, or even workout at home using online tutorials or videos.

Another common unnecessary service is cable TV. With the rise of streaming services, many people find that they can get all the entertainment they need without a traditional cable subscription. If you find that you rarely watch cable TV, consider canceling your subscription and switching to a streaming service or even an antenna to access local channels.

In conclusion, canceling unnecessary services is an important step in reducing your monthly expenses and simplifying your life. By evaluating each service, you subscribe to, reviewing the cancellation process, and standing firm in your decision to cancel, you can save money and reduce stress. Remember, it is okay to let go of services that no longer provide value, and you may even find that you don't miss them at all.

Cut down your cell phone or internet bill.

Instead of cancelling your subscriptions and services, you can also save money by cutting down the recurring costs. A recurring expense that most people have is their cell phone or internet bill. With the rise of smartphones and other gadgets, it's easy to rack up hundreds of dollars in phone and internet bills every month. However, with some simple tips and tricks, it is possible to reduce your monthly bills without sacrificing quality.

The first step to reducing your cell phone or internet bill is to evaluate your usage. Take a look at your monthly statement and see how much data you're using, how many texts and calls you're making, and what features you're paying for. Often, people are paying for more than they need, such as unlimited data when they only use a fraction of it. By scaling back on your plan and only paying for what you use, you can significantly reduce your bill.

Another way to reduce your bill is to negotiate with your provider. Many people don't realize that their cell phone or internet provider is willing to negotiate on pricing, especially if you're a long-time customer. Call your provider and ask if there are any promotions or discounts available. If they say no, don't be afraid to negotiate further or threaten to switch providers. Often, providers are willing to give discounts to keep their customers happy.

One of the most effective ways to reduce your cell phone or internet bill is to bundle services. Many providers offer discounts if you combine your internet, cell phone, and cable or satellite TV services. By bundling, you can save a significant amount of money each month. However, before signing up for a bundle, make sure you'll use all the services included; otherwise, it might end up costing you more.

Another way to reduce your internet bill is to switch providers. Often, people stick with the same provider out of convenience, but switching to a new provider can save you money. Research the different providers in your area and compare their prices and services. You might find that a new provider offers faster internet speeds or more features for a lower price.

Similarly, you can reduce your cell phone bill by switching to a different provider or plan. Many smaller providers offer lower prices and more flexibility than the major carriers. Before switching, make sure to research the provider's coverage and compare prices with your current provider.

Another way to save money on your cell phone bill is to avoid paying for unnecessary features or add-ons. For example, many people pay for insurance on their phone, which can cost up to $10 per month. Instead, consider putting that money aside each month in case you need to replace your phone. Similarly, avoid paying for extra features like ringback tones, which can add up over time.

Finally, consider downgrading your phone or internet package. Many people feel pressured to have the latest and greatest technology, but often, older models or slower internet speeds are more than enough for everyday use. By downgrading your package, you can save money each month without sacrificing much in terms of quality.

In conclusion, there are several ways to reduce your cell phone or internet bill without sacrificing quality or convenience. By evaluating your usage, negotiating with your provider, bundling services, switching providers, avoiding unnecessary features, and downgrading your package, you can save a significant amount of money each month. Remember to research your options thoroughly and don't be afraid to negotiate or switch providers if necessary. With some effort and planning, you can significantly reduce your monthly bills and put that extra money towards other expenses or savings.

Cut down on your electricity and water bills by conserving energy and water.

In many parts of the world, energy and water are becoming increasingly scarce resources. The growing population and industrialization are putting more pressure on these resources, leading to higher prices and a negative impact on the environment. Cutting down on your electricity and water bills not only saves you money, but it also contributes to preserving these precious resources. In this chapter, we will discuss some ways you can conserve energy and water to reduce your bills.

Firstly, you can reduce your electricity bills by using energy-efficient appliances and light bulbs. Most of the energy used in a home is from heating and cooling, followed by appliances and lighting. Therefore, using appliances with high energy ratings and replacing incandescent light bulbs with LED bulbs can make a significant difference in your energy bills. Energy-efficient appliances and light bulbs use less electricity, which means you will be paying less on your monthly electricity bill.

Secondly, you can conserve energy by reducing your energy usage. Simple actions like turning off lights when you leave a room, unplugging electronics when they are not in use, and using natural light instead of artificial lighting can reduce your electricity bill. Additionally, you can take advantage of natural ventilation instead of air conditioning, especially during moderate weather conditions.

Thirdly, you can reduce your water bills by using water-efficient fixtures and appliances. You can install low-flow showerheads, faucets, and toilets to reduce water usage. Additionally, you can fix any water leaks in your home promptly. A leaking faucet can waste gallons of water every day, leading to higher bills. You can also conserve water by taking shorter showers, using a dishwasher instead of washing dishes by hand, and only doing laundry when you have a full load.

Fourthly, you can conserve water by using graywater. Graywater is wastewater from sources like showers, sinks, and washing machines, which can be used for irrigation and other non-potable uses. You can install a graywater system in your home, which will recycle water and reduce the amount of freshwater you use for irrigation or flushing toilets.

Fifthly, you can consider installing solar panels to generate electricity for your home. Solar panels are a great way to reduce your electricity bills and make your home more sustainable. Although the initial cost of installation may be high, you will recoup your investment over time through lower energy bills. Additionally, many states and countries offer incentives and tax credits for homeowners who install solar panels, making it a more cost-effective investment.

In conclusion, conserving energy and water is an effective way to cut down on your electricity and water bills. By using energy-efficient appliances, reducing energy usage, using water-efficient fixtures and appliances, fixing leaks, using graywater, and installing solar panels, you can significantly reduce your monthly bills. These simple steps also contribute to the preservation of precious resources, making it a win-win situation for you and the environment.

Buy used things.

Nowadays, a lot of things seem to be disposable and easily replaceable. It's easy to forget that buying used items can be a great way to save money. Whether you're looking for clothing, furniture, or electronics, there are many benefits to buying used.

First and foremost, buying used items can save you a significant amount of money. Used items are often sold at a fraction of the price of new items, which means you can get what you need without breaking the bank. This is especially useful if you're on a tight budget or looking to make the most of your money.

In addition to being cost-effective, buying used items is also a sustainable choice. By purchasing second-hand goods, you're helping to reduce waste and conserve resources. This is because producing new items requires a lot of energy and resources, which can have a negative impact on the environment. By buying used, you're giving new life to items that might otherwise end up in a landfill.

Another benefit of buying used items is that you can often find unique and interesting pieces that you wouldn't be able to find in a store. Whether you're looking for vintage clothing, antique furniture, or collectibles, the used market can be a treasure trove of unique items that you won't find anywhere else.

So, how can you make the most of buying used items? Here are some tips:

1. Do your research: Before you start shopping for used items, do your research to find out what you're looking for and what a fair price is. This will help you avoid overpaying for items and ensure that you're getting a good deal.

2. Shop around: Don't settle for the first used item you come across. Instead, shop around to find the best deals and the highest quality items.

3. Check for quality: When buying used items, it's important to check for quality. Make sure that the item is in good condition and that it will meet your needs.

4. Ask questions: If you're buying from a seller, don't be afraid to ask questions. Ask about the item's history, how it was used, and any issues it might have.

5. Consider the cost of repairs: If you're buying used electronics or appliances, consider the cost of repairs. While the item might be cheaper upfront, it could end

up costing you more in the long run if you need to pay for repairs.

6. Use online marketplaces: Online marketplaces like eBay and Craigslist can be great places to find used items. Just be sure to take precautions to avoid scams and ensure that you're buying from a reputable seller.

7. Attend garage sales and thrift stores: Garage sales and thrift stores are great places to find used items at a low cost. Just be prepared to do some digging to find the gems.

Overall, buying used items can be a great way to save money, reduce waste, and find unique and interesting items. With a little research and some patience, you can make the most of the used market and find the items you need without breaking the bank.

Sell things you don't need.

In addition to the previous chapter, you can also save money if you sell (used) things, you don't need anymore. Do you have items in your home that you don't use or need? Perhaps you have old clothes, books, or electronics gathering dust in a closet or drawer. Instead of letting these items take up space in your home, why not sell them and make some extra cash? Selling things you don't need can be a great way to declutter your home, earn money, and even help the environment.

First, take a look around your home and identify items that you no longer use or need. This could include clothes that no longer fit, books you've already read, or electronics that have been replaced by newer models. Once you've identified these items, it's time to decide how to sell them.

One option is to sell your items online. There are many websites and apps that make it easy to sell your belongings to people in your area or even around the world. Popular online marketplaces include eBay, Amazon, and Craigslist. You can also use social media platforms like Facebook or Instagram to sell your items to people in your network.

When selling items online, it's important to take clear, well-lit photos of your items and write detailed descriptions that accurately reflect their condition. Be honest about any flaws or damage, as this will help you build trust with potential buyers.

Another option is to sell your items in person at a yard sale or flea market. This can be a great way to get rid of a large number of items all at once, and it can be a fun way to spend a weekend. To host a successful yard sale or flea market booth, be sure to advertise your sale in advance and price your items competitively. Consider grouping similar items together and offering bulk discounts to encourage shoppers to buy more.

If you have high-value items, such as designer clothes or electronics, you may want to consider consigning them at a local thrift store or consignment shop. Consignment shops will sell your items for you and take a percentage of the sale price as a commission. This can be a good option if you don't have the time or energy to sell your items yourself.

Selling things you don't need can be a great way to earn some extra money, but it's important to be realistic about how much money you can make. While you may be able to get a good price for some items, others may not be worth much at all. Be prepared to sell some items for a low price or even give them away for free if you can't find a buyer.

In addition to earning extra money, selling things you don't need can also be good for the environment. When you sell your items, you're keeping them out of the landfill and giving them a second life with someone else who will use and appreciate them. This is a great way to reduce waste and promote sustainability.

Finally, selling things you don't need can be a great way to declutter your home and reduce stress. When you have a lot of unnecessary items in your home, it can be hard to relax and focus on the things that really matter. By selling your items and creating a more streamlined living space, you'll free up mental and physical space that can be used for more important things.

In conclusion, selling things you don't need can be a great way to earn extra money, help the environment, and declutter your home. Whether you sell your items online, in person, or through a consignment shop, be sure to take clear photos and write accurate descriptions to help your items sell quickly. With a little effort, you can turn your clutter into cash and enjoy a more organized, stress-free home.

Visit thrift stores.

Shopping at thrift stores has become increasingly popular in recent years, and for good reason. Not only do they offer a wide variety of unique and affordable items, but they also provide an eco-friendly and sustainable shopping option. In this chapter, we will explore the benefits of shopping at thrift stores and provide tips for making the most out of your thrift store experience.

Thrift stores, also known as second-hand stores, offer a range of items including clothing, furniture, home decor, and electronics. These items are usually donated by individuals or organizations, and are sold at a significantly lower price than retail stores. This makes thrift stores a great option for those who are budget-conscious or looking for a sustainable shopping alternative.

One of the biggest advantages of shopping at thrift stores is the affordability of the items. Clothing, in particular, can be found at a fraction of the cost of new items. This is especially beneficial for those who are looking to update their wardrobe without breaking the bank. Additionally, thrift stores often carry vintage or unique items that cannot be found in mainstream retail stores, making it an ideal shopping destination for those looking to express their individual style.

Aside from the cost-saving benefits, shopping at thrift stores also supports a sustainable and eco-friendly lifestyle. By purchasing second-hand items, you are reducing the amount of waste produced by the fashion and retail industries. It also prevents items from being sent to landfills, which in turn reduces the carbon footprint and conserves natural resources.

However, shopping at thrift stores can be overwhelming for those who are new to the experience. It's important to go into a thrift store with an open mind and a clear idea of what you are looking for. Here are some tips for making the most out of your thrift store shopping experience:

1. Have a plan: Before heading to the thrift store, make a list of the items you are looking for. This will help you stay focused and avoid impulse purchases. It's also helpful to have an idea of the sizes and styles you are looking for to avoid spending too much time sifting through items that won't work for you.

2. Check for quality: While thrift stores offer great deals, it's important to ensure the items you are purchasing are still in good condition. Take the time to inspect clothing for tears, stains, and signs of wear. For furniture, check for stability and any damage. Electronics should be tested before purchasing to ensure they are in working condition.

3. Take your time: Thrift stores can be overwhelming with their large selection of items. Take your time and browse through each section carefully. It's also a good idea to check back frequently, as new items are added regularly.

4. Be creative: Thrift stores offer a unique opportunity to get creative with your style and home decor. Don't be afraid to mix and match items to create a one-of-a-kind look. You may be surprised at what you can find and how it can be repurposed.

5. Give back: Consider donating items that you no longer need or use to thrift stores. Not only does this support the cycle of sustainable shopping, but it also provides support to those in need.

In conclusion, shopping at thrift stores is a great way to save money, support sustainability, and add unique items to your wardrobe and home decor. With these tips in mind, you can make the most out of your thrift store experience and enjoy the benefits of second-hand shopping.

## Savings apps.

As a disclaimer – I am not sponsored by any company and this book does not contain any affiliate links. But because I wrote several times about savings apps, I decided to give these their own chapter. Please be aware, that these my change and that in the moment you are reading this, there might be new and better ones out there. I strongly advise you to do your own research before choosing one.

A savings app is a digital tool designed to help you save money, manage your budget, and track your expenses. With these apps, you can set goals, create budgets, track your progress, and get tips on how to save more money.

One of the main benefits of using a savings app is that it makes it easier to track your expenses. With most savings apps, you can link your bank account and credit cards to the app, and it will automatically track your spending. This makes it easier to see where your money is going and identify areas where you can cut back.

Another benefit of using a savings app is that it can help you set and achieve financial goals. For example, you can set a goal to save a certain amount of money each month, and the app will help you track your progress and stay on track. Some savings apps also offer rewards for reaching your goals, such as cashback or gift cards.

There are many different types of savings apps available, so it's important to find one that works for you. Some popular savings apps include:

1. Mint: Mint is a free app that allows you to track your expenses, create budgets, and set financial goals. It also offers personalized financial advice and insights to help you save more money.

2. Acorns: Acorns is a savings app that automatically invests your spare change in a diversified portfolio of stocks and bonds. It also offers a retirement account and a checking account with no minimum balance or monthly fees.

3. Digit: Digit is a savings app that analyzes your spending habits and automatically saves money for you. It also offers a feature called "Goals," which allows you to set savings goals and track your progress.

4. Qapital: Qapital is a savings app that allows you to set up rules for saving money. For example, you can set a rule to save $5 every time you buy a coffee. It also offers a feature called "Goals," which allows you to set savings goals and track your progress.

5. Stash: Stash is a savings app that allows you to invest in stocks and ETFs with as little as $5. It also offers a checking account with no minimum balance or monthly fees.

When choosing a savings app, it's important to consider the fees and features of each app. Some apps charge fees for certain features, such as investment accounts, while others are completely free. It's also important to read reviews and do your research to ensure that the app is reputable and secure.

In conclusion, using a savings app can be a great way to manage your finances, track your expenses, and achieve your financial goals. With so many different savings apps available, it's important to find one that works for you and fits your financial needs. By using a savings app, you can take control of your finances and start saving more money today.

Use a cash flow projection tool to manage your finances.

This is another tool that can you help getting a better overview on what's going on inside your account and wallet. Managing your finances can seem like a daunting task, especially when you have multiple sources of income, bills to pay, and savings goals to work towards. One tool that can make this process easier is a cash flow projection tool.

A cash flow projection tool is a spreadsheet or software that helps you manage your finances by forecasting your cash inflows and outflows over a given period. By using this tool, you can create a plan for your income and expenses, and track how well you're sticking to that plan.

Here are some tips for using a cash flow projection tool effectively:

1. Start with accurate data: To use a cash flow projection tool, you need to have an accurate picture of your income and expenses. Make sure you have all your financial information in one place, including your income sources, bills, and other expenses.

2. Be realistic: When creating your cash flow projection, be realistic about your income and expenses. Don't overestimate your income or underestimate your expenses, as this will result in an inaccurate projection. Be conservative in your estimates, and adjust them as necessary.

3. Include one-time expenses: Many people make the mistake of only including recurring expenses in their cash flow projection. However, it's important to also

include one-time expenses, such as home repairs or car maintenance. These expenses can have a significant impact on your cash flow, so it's important to plan for them.

4. Review and adjust regularly: Your financial situation can change quickly, so it's important to review and adjust your cash flow projection regularly. This will help you stay on track and make adjustments as needed.

Now that you understand the basics of using a cash flow projection tool, let's dive into the benefits of using one:

1. Helps you plan for the future: A cash flow projection tool allows you to plan for future expenses and income. This can help you avoid unexpected expenses and make the most of your income.

2. Helps you manage your cash flow: By tracking your cash inflows and outflows, you can better manage your cash flow. This can help you avoid overdraft fees, late fees, and other unnecessary expenses.

3. Helps you make informed decisions: When you have a clear picture of your financial situation, you can make more informed decisions about your finances. For example, you may be able to see that you need to cut

back on certain expenses to achieve your savings goals.

4. Helps you identify potential problems: By regularly reviewing your cash flow projection, you can identify potential problems before they become major issues. For example, you may notice that your expenses are consistently higher than your income, which could indicate that you need to make some changes to your spending habits.

Now that you know the benefits of using a cash flow projection tool, let's look at some tips for using it effectively:

1. Use it regularly: To get the most out of your cash flow projection tool, you should use it regularly. This will help you stay on top of your finances and make adjustments as necessary.

2. Be realistic: As mentioned earlier, it's important to be realistic when creating your cash flow projection. This will help you avoid overestimating your income or underestimating your expenses.

3. Keep it simple: While some cash flow projection tools can be quite complex, it's important to keep it simple. A simple spreadsheet or software can be just as effective as a more complex tool.

4.  Use it to set goals: Your cash flow projection tool can help you set financial goals and track your progress towards those goals. This can be a great motivator and can help you stay on track with your finances.

In conclusion, using a cash flow projection tool is an effective way to manage your finances and achieve your financial goals. By tracking your income and expenses, you can identify areas where you may be overspending and adjust your budget accordingly. This tool also helps you to anticipate cash flow shortages and plan for unexpected expenses.

Utilize public transportation or carpooling.

Transportation expenses can add up quickly, especially for those who rely on personal vehicles to commute or travel regularly. However, there are several ways to reduce these expenses, and one of the most effective ways is to use public transportation or carpool.

Using public transportation, such as buses or trains, can be a cost-effective alternative to driving a personal vehicle. Public transportation systems are designed to transport large numbers of people at once, which makes them an environmentally friendly and budget-friendly option. In most cities, public transportation fares are much cheaper than the cost of fuel, parking, and maintenance for a personal vehicle.

Another option is carpooling, which involves sharing a ride with other commuters who are traveling in the same direction. Carpooling can significantly reduce transportation expenses by sharing fuel costs and reducing wear and tear on personal vehicles. Additionally, carpooling can reduce traffic congestion and help reduce carbon emissions, making it a more environmentally friendly option.

Here are some tips for reducing transportation expenses by using public transportation or carpooling:

1. Research public transportation options in your area: Most cities have a public transportation system that includes buses, trains, and subways. Research the available options in your area to determine which ones are the most convenient and cost-effective for your needs. Look for discounts for frequent riders, students, and seniors.

2. Plan your commute ahead of time: If you're planning to use public transportation, plan your commute ahead of time. Research schedules, routes, and stops to make sure you know when and where to catch your ride. This will help you avoid missed connections and ensure that you arrive at your destination on time.

3. Consider carpooling with coworkers: If you have coworkers who live near you or on the way to your workplace, consider carpooling with them. This can reduce transportation costs and provide an opportunity for social interaction during your commute. Use apps like Uber Pool or Waze Carpool to find potential carpool partners.

4. Join a ridesharing community: There are several ridesharing communities and apps that allow you to connect with people who are traveling in the same direction. This can be a great way to reduce transportation costs, meet new people, and reduce

your carbon footprint. Some popular apps include BlaBlaCar, Ridejoy, and Carma.

5. Opt for walking or biking: For short distances, consider walking or biking instead of using a personal vehicle or public transportation. This can be a great way to reduce transportation costs, improve your health, and reduce your carbon footprint. In addition, many cities have bike-share programs that allow you to rent a bike for a short period of time at a low cost.

Overall, using public transportation or carpooling can be an effective way to reduce transportation expenses. By doing your research, planning ahead, and considering alternative modes of transportation, you can save money, reduce your carbon footprint, and improve your overall transportation experience.

Walk or bike.

Transportation expenses can be a significant burden on our wallets, but there are ways to reduce them. One of the best ways to do so is by walking or biking. Not only can it save you money, but it's also good for your health and the environment. In this chapter, we will discuss the benefits of walking or biking, how to make it a part of your daily routine, and tips to ensure your safety while on the road.

Benefits of walking or biking:

There are numerous benefits to walking or biking, both for your wallet and your health. Firstly, walking or biking is free. You don't need to worry about paying for gas or parking, which can add up quickly. Secondly, it's a great way to get exercise. Walking or biking can help you maintain a healthy weight, reduce your risk of chronic disease, and improve your mood.

Thirdly, walking or biking is good for the environment. Cars are one of the largest contributors to greenhouse gas emissions, so by walking or biking, you're doing your part to reduce your carbon footprint. Finally, walking or biking can be a great way to de-stress and clear your mind. Taking a few minutes to get outside and move your body can do wonders for your mental health.

Making it a part of your routine:

Incorporating walking or biking into your daily routine can be easier than you think. Firstly, consider the distance of your commute. If it's a relatively short distance, walking or biking may be a feasible option. Secondly, plan your route in advance. Map out the best route that is safe and has the least amount of traffic. Thirdly, set aside enough time. Walking or biking may take longer than driving, so make sure you allow enough time to get to your destination.

Finally, invest in the right equipment. If you plan on biking, make sure you have a bike that is comfortable and reliable. If you plan on walking, invest in comfortable shoes and appropriate clothing.

Tips for staying safe:

While walking or biking can be a great way to save money and get exercise, it's important to take safety precautions to ensure you arrive at your destination safely. Firstly, always wear a helmet if you plan on biking. It can reduce your risk of head injury in the event of an accident.

Secondly, always obey traffic laws. This includes stopping at stop signs, signaling when turning, and obeying traffic lights. Thirdly, make sure you are visible. Wear bright colors or reflective clothing, especially if you are biking at night. Fourthly, be aware of your surroundings. Stay alert and avoid distractions, such as using your phone while on the road.

Finally, consider joining a walking or biking group. Not only can it be a great way to meet new people, but it can also provide an extra layer of safety. You'll be biking or walking with a group of people, which can make you more visible to drivers.

Conclusion:

Walking or biking is a great way to reduce your transportation expenses. It's free, good for your health, and good for the environment. By making it a part of your daily routine and taking safety precautions, you can enjoy the benefits of walking or biking without compromising your safety. Start by mapping out your route, investing in the right equipment, and considering joining a walking or biking group. With a little planning and preparation, you'll be on your way to a healthier, more cost-effective lifestyle.

Drive a fuel-efficient car.

With the recent surge of gas prices, fuel-efficient cars can be more relevant than ever for your wallet. Driving a fuel-efficient car is one of the best ways to save money on transportation costs. A fuel-efficient car uses less gas, which means you'll spend less money at the pump. In addition, these cars often have lower emissions, which can be good for the environment. But what exactly is a fuel-efficient car, and how can you find one?

First, it's important to understand what fuel efficiency means. Fuel efficiency is a measure of how far a car can travel on a gallon of gas. The higher the fuel efficiency, the farther the car can go on a single tank of gas. There are a few ways to measure fuel efficiency, but the most common is miles per gallon (MPG).

When shopping for a fuel-efficient car, it's important to look for one with a high MPG rating. The Environmental Protection Agency (EPA) provides fuel efficiency ratings for all new cars sold in the United States. These ratings are based on standardized tests that simulate typical driving conditions. The EPA ratings can be a good starting point for finding a fuel-efficient car, but it's important to keep in mind that your actual MPG may vary depending on your driving habits and conditions.

In addition to the EPA ratings, there are a few other factors to consider when looking for a fuel-efficient car. First, smaller cars are generally more fuel-efficient than larger ones. This is because smaller cars have less weight to carry, which means they require less energy to move. Second, cars with hybrid or electric engines are typically more fuel-efficient than those with traditional gasoline engines. Hybrid cars use a combination of gasoline and electricity to power the vehicle, while electric cars run entirely on electricity.

Once you've found a fuel-efficient car that meets your needs, there are a few things you can do to maximize your savings. One of the most important is to keep your car properly maintained. Regular maintenance, such as oil changes and tire rotations, can help keep your car running smoothly and efficiently. In addition, make sure you're using the right type of oil and keeping your tires properly inflated.

Another way to save money on transportation costs is to drive more efficiently. This means avoiding aggressive driving, such as speeding and sudden stops, which can use up more gas. Instead, try to maintain a steady speed and anticipate stops ahead of time. Also, avoid idling your car for long periods of time, as this can waste gas.

If you're not in the market for a new car, there are still ways to improve the fuel efficiency of your current vehicle. One of the easiest is to reduce the amount of weight you're carrying. This means removing any unnecessary items from your car, such as heavy tools or luggage. In addition, try to combine trips and plan your routes to minimize driving time.

Finally, consider carpooling or using public transportation when possible. Carpooling is a great way to share the costs of transportation with others, and many cities have carpool lanes that can help you save time on your commute. Public transportation, such as buses and trains, can also be a cost-effective option for getting around.

In conclusion, driving a fuel-efficient car is a great way to save money on transportation costs. By choosing a car with a high MPG rating and maintaining it properly, you can maximize your savings and reduce your environmental impact. In addition, driving more efficiently, reducing weight, and carpooling or using public transportation can all help you save money on transportation costs.

# Chapter 3 – Financial education.

First of all, I want to congratulate you. Why? Simply because you are reading this, you did one of the major steps in the direction of financial freedom: education.

Financial education is a crucial aspect of personal finance management. It involves gaining knowledge and skills necessary to make informed decisions about money matters. Unfortunately, many people lack sufficient financial education, leading to poor financial decisions that result in financial stress, debt, and insecurity. A lack of financial literacy can also lead to missed opportunities to grow wealth and achieve financial goals.

It is essential for people of all ages and backgrounds, as it enables them to understand financial concepts, such as budgeting, investing, and debt management. It also helps individuals to learn how to create a financial plan that aligns with their goals, values, and lifestyles. By gaining financial education, individuals can make informed decisions about their money, leading to better financial outcomes.

Moreover, financial education can help individuals avoid common financial mistakes, such as overspending, not saving enough, and taking on too much debt. It can also help individuals to develop good financial habits, such as tracking their expenses, creating a budget, and setting financial goals. By practicing these habits, individuals can achieve financial stability, reduce financial stress, and build long-term wealth.

In today's world, where the financial landscape is constantly changing, and individuals are faced with complex financial products and services, it is crucial. Without proper financial education, individuals may fall prey to scams or make uninformed decisions that can lead to financial hardship.

In this chapter, we will explore the importance of financial education and how it can benefit individuals in their personal finance management. We will discuss the basic concepts of financial education, such as budgeting, saving, investing, and debt management. We will also provide practical tips on how individuals can gain financial education, such as through books, online resources, and courses. By the end of this chapter, readers will have a better understanding of the importance of financial education and the steps they can take to improve their financial literacy.

Read books about finance.

Again, you already adapted this habit. But I can tell you, that there are many more great books out there. Having a solid understanding of finance is essential for building a secure financial future. However, the world of finance can be overwhelming and complex, making it difficult to know where to start. Fortunately, there are many excellent books available that can help individuals improve their financial literacy, regardless of their income level or experience.

One book that is particularly useful for beginners and intermediates is "The Simple Path to Wealth" by JL Collins. This book is an easy-to-read guide that provides practical advice on investing and achieving financial independence. Collins explains complex financial concepts in simple terms and offers actionable advice that readers can implement immediately. The book is particularly helpful for those who are just starting to invest and want to learn how to do so intelligently.

Another great book to start with is "Your Money or Your Life" by Vicki Robin and Joe Dominguez. This book focuses on the importance of financial independence and offers practical steps for achieving it. The authors stress the importance of mindful spending and tracking expenses, and provide strategies for saving and investing for the future. The book is particularly helpful for those who want to gain control over their finances and build a more secure financial future.

For those interested in personal finance and budgeting, "The Total Money Makeover" by Dave Ramsey is an excellent choice. Ramsey offers a step-by-step guide to getting out of debt and building wealth. He provides practical advice on budgeting, saving, and investing, and offers motivational stories and success stories from people who have successfully followed his plan. The book is particularly helpful for those who are struggling with debt and want to learn how to manage their money more effectively.

"Rich Dad Poor Dad" by Robert Kiyosaki is another great book for beginners. This book offers a unique perspective on personal finance and focuses on the importance of building passive income streams. Kiyosaki shares stories from his own life and provides practical advice for building wealth and achieving financial freedom. The book is particularly helpful for those who are interested in real estate investing and want to learn more about building passive income streams.

Finally, "The Millionaire Next Door" by Thomas J. Stanley and William D. Danko is an excellent book for beginners who want to learn more about wealth accumulation and building wealth over time. The authors conducted extensive research on millionaires and found that many of them had modest incomes and lived frugally. The book provides practical advice on building wealth over time and offers strategies for living below one's means and building wealth through investing.

In conclusion, reading books about finance is an excellent way to improve one's financial literacy and build a more secure financial future. Whether you are a beginner or have some experience in finance, there are many great books available that can help you improve your financial knowledge and make smarter decisions about money.

Learn about finance online.

The internet has made it easier than ever before to learn about finance from the comfort of your own home. There are many websites, blogs, and forums dedicated to teaching people about personal finance, investing, and money management. Whether you are a complete beginner or have some knowledge already, there are resources available online that can help you improve your financial literacy.

One of the most popular ways to learn about finance online is through personal finance blogs. There are many bloggers who share their own experiences with managing money, investing, and building wealth. Some of the best blogs offer practical advice and tips that can be applied to your own financial situation. Some of the top personal finance blogs include The Simple Dollar, Mr. Money Mustache, and Get Rich Slowly.

Another great way to learn about finance online is through financial education websites. These websites provide a wide range of resources, including articles, videos, and calculators, to help you improve your financial literacy. Some of the top financial education websites include Investopedia, NerdWallet, and The Balance.

Online courses are another popular option for learning about finance. There are many courses available that cover a variety of topics, including personal finance, investing, and financial planning. Some of the most popular online course providers include Coursera, Udemy, and edX.

Podcasts are also a great way to learn about finance on-the-go. Many finance podcasts feature interviews with experts, discussions about current financial news and events, and practical tips for managing your money. Some of the top finance podcasts include The Dave Ramsey Show, The BiggerPockets Money Podcast, and So Money with Farnoosh Torabi.

Social media can also be a valuable resource for learning about finance. There are many personal finance influencers on platforms like Twitter, Instagram, and YouTube who share their own experiences and offer tips and advice for managing money. Some of the top personal finance influencers include Ramit Sethi, Suze Orman, and Michelle Singletary.

One important thing to keep in mind when learning about finance online is to make sure that the sources you are using are reputable and trustworthy. There is a lot of misinformation and scams out there, so it's important to do your research and verify the information you are receiving.

In addition, it's important to remember that personal finance is a complex and ever-evolving field. While online resources can be helpful, they should not be your only source of financial education. It's also important to seek advice from financial professionals, such as financial advisors or certified public accountants, who can provide personalized guidance based on your specific financial situation.

In conclusion, learning about finance online is a great way to improve your financial literacy and take control of your money. There are many resources available, including blogs, websites, courses, podcasts, and social media influencers, that can provide valuable information and advice. However, it's important to make sure that the sources you are using are reputable and to seek advice from financial professionals as needed. By taking advantage of online resources and seeking expert advice, you can improve your financial knowledge and make informed decisions about your money.

Financial seminars.

Take this chapter with a grain of salt — unnecessary spendings and subscriptions are very close here and there are many people that seemingly want to help you but all they want is your money. In the following, we want to focus on either free seminars or such that you will actually benefit from.

Attending financial seminars is a great way to gain valuable knowledge and insights into managing your finances effectively. Whether you're just starting out on your financial journey or looking to improve your existing skills, attending financial seminars can help you learn from experts in the field and gain valuable insights into managing your money.

One of the biggest benefits of attending financial seminars is that you can learn from experts who have years of experience in managing their finances. These experts can share their experiences, tips, and strategies for managing money effectively, which can be immensely helpful for those looking to improve their financial situation.

Financial seminars can cover a wide range of topics, including budgeting, saving, investing, and retirement planning. By attending these seminars, you can learn about a variety of financial topics and gain a better understanding of how to manage your money effectively.

There are many financial seminars available, both online and in person, so it's important to choose the right one for your needs. Look for seminars that are relevant to your financial goals and that are led by experienced professionals in the field.

Many financial seminars are free, while others may require a fee to attend. However, the cost of attending a seminar is often well worth it, as the knowledge and insights you gain can help you save money and improve your financial situation in the long run.

In addition to learning from experts in the field, attending financial seminars can also provide networking opportunities. You can meet other like-minded individuals who are also interested in improving their financial situation, which can be a great way to exchange ideas and learn from each other.

Another benefit of attending financial seminars is that you can ask questions and get personalized advice from experts. This can be particularly helpful if you're facing a specific financial challenge and need guidance on how to overcome it.

When attending financial seminars, it's important to come prepared with questions and a willingness to learn. Take notes during the seminar and ask for clarification if you're unsure about something. Remember, the more you learn, the better equipped you'll be to manage your finances effectively.

In conclusion, attending financial seminars is a valuable way to gain knowledge and insights into managing your finances effectively. Whether you're just starting out or looking to improve your existing skills, attending financial seminars can help you learn from experts in the field, gain valuable insights, and network with like-minded individuals. Other seminars you could attempt, are tax seminars. We will therefore talk about tax plannings in the next chapter.

Learn about tax planning.

Tax planning is an important aspect of personal finance that often goes overlooked. Taxes can take a significant chunk out of your income, so learning how to plan and optimize your tax strategy can help you keep more of your hard-earned money. In this chapter, we will discuss the importance of tax planning and provide some tips and resources to help you get started.

Understanding Taxes:

Before we dive into tax planning strategies, it's important to understand how taxes work. Taxes are a way for the government to generate revenue to fund public services and programs. The amount of tax you pay is determined by your income, deductions, and credits. Tax rates can vary based on your income level and filing status. There are different types of taxes as well, including federal income tax, state income tax, and payroll taxes, among others.

Tax Planning Strategies:

Now that you have a basic understanding of how taxes work, let's discuss some tax planning strategies that can help you reduce your tax liability and keep more of your money.

1. Maximize Your Deductions and Credits:

One of the most effective ways to reduce your tax liability is to take advantage of deductions and credits. Deductions are expenses that you can subtract from your taxable income, while credits are dollar-for-dollar reductions of your tax liability. Some common deductions and credits include charitable contributions, mortgage interest, education expenses, and retirement contributions. Make sure to keep track of all your eligible expenses throughout the year and work with a tax professional to ensure you are claiming all the deductions and credits you are entitled to.

2. Contribute to Retirement Accounts:

Contributing to a retirement account, such as a 401(k) or IRA, can have significant tax benefits. These contributions are typically tax-deductible, which means they reduce your taxable income. Additionally, any investment gains within the account are tax-deferred until you withdraw them in retirement, which can also provide significant tax savings. Make sure to research the different types of retirement accounts available and choose one that aligns with your financial goals.

3. Plan Your Investments Wisely:

Investments can have significant tax implications, so it's important to plan them strategically. For example, holding investments for more than one year can qualify you for lower long-term capital gains tax rates. Additionally, investing in tax-advantaged accounts, such as a Health Savings Account (HSA) or a 529 college savings plan, can provide additional tax benefits.

4. Consider Tax-Loss Harvesting:

Tax-loss harvesting is a strategy where you sell investments that have decreased in value to offset capital gains tax on other investments. This strategy can help reduce your tax liability and can be especially effective during times of market volatility. However, it's important to consult with a financial professional before implementing this strategy to ensure it aligns with your overall investment strategy.

Resources for Learning About Tax Planning:

There are many resources available to help you learn more about tax planning. Here are some beginner-friendly books and websites that can help you get started:

1. "Taxes Made Simple: Income Taxes Explained in 100 Pages or Less" by Mike Piper: This book provides a

straightforward overview of how taxes work and strategies for reducing your tax liability.

2. IRS.gov: The IRS website provides a wealth of information on tax planning, including forms and publications, tax calculators, and tax law updates.

3. TurboTax: TurboTax is a popular tax preparation software that can help you navigate the tax filing process and maximize your deductions and credits.

4. Investopedia: Investopedia is a website that provides educational resources on personal finance, including tax planning strategies.

Conclusion:

In conclusion, tax planning is an important aspect of personal finance that can help you minimize your tax liability and maximize your savings. By understanding the basics of tax planning and taking steps to implement effective strategies, you can keep more of your hard-earned money in your pocket. Whether you choose to work with a tax professional or learn on your own through books, seminars, and online resources, taking the time to educate yourself on tax planning is a wise investment in your financial future.

Learn about interest rates.

Interest rates are a critical component of the financial world, and understanding how they work is essential for anyone who wants to make informed financial decisions. Whether you are looking to buy a home, invest in stocks, or simply open a savings account, interest rates will have a significant impact on your financial well-being.

Put simply, interest rates are the cost of borrowing money. When you borrow money, you agree to pay back the loan amount plus interest over a set period. The interest rate determines the amount of interest you will pay, and it can vary depending on several factors, including the type of loan, the lender, and your creditworthiness.

There are two main types of interest rates: fixed and variable. Fixed interest rates remain the same for the duration of the loan, while variable interest rates can change over time based on market conditions. Both types have their advantages and disadvantages, and it's important to understand them before making any financial decisions.

One of the most significant factors affecting interest rates is inflation. Inflation refers to the rate at which the general level of prices for goods and services is rising. When inflation is high, interest rates tend to be high as well because lenders want to be compensated for the loss of value in their money over time. When inflation is low, interest rates tend to be low as well because lenders don't need as much compensation for the loss of value.

Another important concept related to interest rates is compounding. Compounding refers to the process of earning interest on interest. For example, if you have a savings account that earns 5% interest per year and you leave the interest in the account instead of withdrawing it, you will earn interest on the original balance plus the interest you have already earned. Over time, this can lead to significant growth in your savings.

Learning about interest rates can help you make informed decisions when it comes to borrowing, saving, and investing. If you are looking to take out a loan, it's important to compare interest rates from different lenders to find the best deal. Similarly, if you are looking to save money, it's important to find a savings account or investment vehicle that offers a competitive interest rate.

There are many resources available to help you learn about interest rates, including books, online courses, and financial advisors. Some recommended books for beginners include

"The Simple Path to Wealth" by JL Collins, "The Intelligent Investor" by Benjamin Graham, and "The Total Money Makeover" by Dave Ramsey. Online courses and webinars can also be a great way to learn about interest rates, and many financial advisors offer consultations to help you understand how interest rates can impact your finances.

In conclusion, understanding interest rates is an essential part of financial literacy. Whether you are looking to borrow money, save for the future, or invest in stocks, interest rates will play a significant role in your financial success. By learning about interest rates and how they work, you can make informed decisions and take control of your financial future.

Let's look at a specific scenario:

Let's say you have a credit card with a balance of -$1,000 and an interest rate of 20% per year. If you don't pay off the balance in full at the end of the month, interest will start accruing on the remaining balance.

To calculate the interest for one month, you first need to determine the monthly interest rate. To do this, you divide the annual interest rate by 12 (the number of months in a year). So, in this case, the monthly interest rate would be:

20% / 12 = 1.67%

Next, you multiply the monthly interest rate by the balance to find out how much interest you will be charged for that month:

1.67% x $1,000 = $16.70

So, if you don't pay off the full balance at the end of the month, you will be charged $16.70 in interest for that month. This may not seem like a lot, but if you continue to carry a balance on your credit card, the interest charges can quickly add up and become a significant expense.

It's important to understand how interest rates work so that you can make informed decisions about borrowing money and managing your debt. By taking the time to learn about interest rates, you can avoid costly mistakes and make smarter financial choices.

Learn about compound interest.

Compound interest is a concept that can be a powerful tool for growing your savings and investments over time. Essentially, compound interest is interest that is earned not only on the initial amount of money invested, but also on any interest that has been previously earned. This means that over time, the amount of interest you earn will continue to increase, as long as you leave your money invested.

For example, let's say you invest $1,000 in a savings account that earns 5% interest annually. At the end of the first year, you would earn $50 in interest. But instead of withdrawing that interest, you leave it in the account. In the second year, you would earn 5% interest not only on the initial $1,000, but also on the $50 of interest you earned in the first year. This means you would earn $52.50 in interest in the second year. Over time, this can lead to significant growth in your savings.

One of the benefits of compound interest is that it allows your savings to grow faster than simple interest, which is interest that is only earned on the initial amount of money invested. In the example above, if the interest was simple interest instead of compound interest, you would only earn $50 in interest each year, regardless of how many years you left the money invested.

Understanding compound interest is important not only for saving money, but also for investing. Many investments, such as stocks and mutual funds, also earn compound interest over time. By leaving your investments untouched and allowing the interest to compound, you can potentially earn significant returns over the long term.

However, it's important to note that compound interest can work against you as well. For example, if you have high-interest debt such as credit card debt, the interest charges can compound over time and make it difficult to pay off the balance. This is why it's important to pay off high-interest debt as quickly as possible and avoid taking on new debt whenever possible.

To make the most of compound interest, it's important to start early and be consistent with your saving or investing. The longer you leave your money invested, the more time it has to compound and grow. Additionally, the more you can contribute to your savings or investment account, the more interest you will earn over time.

There are many resources available to help you learn more about compound interest and how to make it work for you. Online calculators can help you see how much your savings or investments could grow over time with compound interest, and financial advisors can provide personalized advice on how to incorporate compound interest into your overall financial plan.

Learn about credit scores.

Understanding credit scores is an essential part of financial education. Your credit score is a three-digit number that represents your creditworthiness, and it can have a significant impact on your ability to borrow money, get a credit card, rent an apartment, or even get a job. If you want to improve your financial health, you need to learn about credit scores and how they work.

Credit scores are calculated based on your credit report, which contains information about your credit history. Your credit report includes details about your loans, credit cards, and other credit accounts, as well as your payment history and the amount of debt you owe. All of this information is used to calculate your credit score, which is typically between 300 and 850.

One of the most critical factors in calculating your credit score is your payment history. Late payments or missed payments can have a significant negative impact on your score, while consistent, on-time payments can help boost your score. Another essential factor is your credit utilization ratio, which is the amount of credit you are using compared to the total credit available to you. Ideally, you want to keep your credit utilization ratio below 30% to maintain a good credit score.

Learning about credit scores can help you take control of your financial health. Here are some things you should know:

1. How to Check Your Credit Score

The first step in improving your credit score is to know where you stand. You can get a free credit report from each of the three major credit bureaus (Equifax, Experian, and TransUnion) once a year. You can also check your credit score for free from many financial institutions or through credit monitoring services.

2. How to Improve Your Credit Score

If you have a low credit score, there are steps you can take to improve it. First, make sure you are making all of your payments on time. Late payments can have a significant negative impact on your score. You should also try to pay down your debt, which can help reduce your credit utilization ratio. Finally, avoid opening new credit accounts or closing existing ones, as this can have a negative impact on your credit score.

3. How Credit Scores Impact Your Life

Your credit score can have a significant impact on your ability to borrow money or get credit cards. It can also affect your ability to rent an apartment, get a job, or even qualify for insurance. Understanding how credit scores impact your life can help motivate you to take steps to improve your score.

4. How to Build Credit

If you have no credit history, it can be challenging to get approved for loans or credit cards. One way to build credit is to get a secured credit card or become an authorized user on someone else's credit card. You can also take out a small personal loan or get a credit-builder loan to establish a credit history.

5. How to Protect Your Credit Score

Identity theft and credit fraud can have a significant impact on your credit score. To protect yourself, you should monitor your credit report regularly and report any suspicious activity to the credit bureaus. You should also be careful about giving out your personal information, especially online.

In conclusion, learning about credit scores is an essential part of financial education. Understanding how credit scores are calculated and how they impact your life can help you make better financial decisions and improve your financial health. By checking your credit score regularly, taking steps to improve your score, and protecting yourself from identity theft and credit fraud, you can take control of your financial future.

Pay off your credit card debt every month.

Since you made it through several helpful tips for saving money, I really hope that you don't use your credit card on a regular basis. However, if you do or if you just jumped to this point, this is a really really important one.

Credit card debt can be one of the biggest financial burdens that people face. High interest rates can quickly pile up, making it difficult to pay off the debt and leaving many feeling trapped in a cycle of debt. However, there is a way to avoid this cycle and become debt-free: paying off your credit card debt every month.

First, it's important to understand how credit card debt works. When you make a purchase with a credit card, you're essentially borrowing money from the credit card company. Each month, you receive a statement that shows your balance, and you have the option to pay off the entire balance or just a portion of it. If you only pay a portion of the balance, interest is charged on the remaining amount.

The interest rate on credit card debt is typically much higher than other types of debt, such as a mortgage or car loan. If you carry a balance from month to month, the interest charges can quickly add up and make it difficult to ever pay off the debt.

To avoid this cycle of debt, it's important to make a plan to pay off your credit card debt in full every month. Here are some tips to help you do so:

1. Create a budget: The first step in paying off your credit card debt is to create a budget. This will help you to see where your money is going and where you can cut back. Look for areas where you can reduce your spending and put that money towards paying off your credit card debt.

2. Use your credit card wisely: Only use your credit card for purchases that you can pay off in full at the end of the month. Avoid using your credit card for large purchases that you can't afford to pay off right away.

3. Pay more than the minimum payment: If you can't pay off your credit card debt in full, be sure to pay more than the minimum payment each month. This will help you to pay off the debt faster and reduce the amount of interest you'll be charged.

4. Consider a balance transfer: If you have a high interest rate on your credit card debt, consider transferring the balance to a credit card with a lower interest rate. This can help you to save money on interest charges and pay off your debt faster.

5. Avoid new debt: While you're paying off your credit card debt, avoid taking on new debt. This will only make it more difficult to pay off your credit card debt in full every month.

6. Track your progress: Keep track of your progress as you pay off your credit card debt. This will help you to stay motivated and see how far you've come.

By paying off your credit card debt in full every month, you can avoid the cycle of debt and improve your financial health. It may take some time and effort, but it's worth it in the long run. With a little discipline and determination, you can become debt-free.

Use a debt payoff strategy, such as the debt snowball or debt avalanche method.

What if you already are struggling with debt? In this chapter we will talk about some of the best known strategies to tackle your debt using the money you saved by living my previous chapters.

One effective strategy is the debt payoff method, which involves prioritizing your debts and paying them off in a strategic order. Two popular debt payoff methods are the debt snowball and debt avalanche method.

The debt snowball method involves paying off your debts from smallest to largest. Start by listing all of your debts in order from smallest to largest. Make the minimum payment on each debt except for the smallest one. On the smallest debt, pay as much as you can afford each month until it is paid off. Once the smallest debt is paid off, move on to the next smallest debt and repeat the process. As you pay off each debt, you will gain momentum and motivation to continue paying off the larger debts.

The debt avalanche method, on the other hand, involves paying off your debts in order from highest interest rate to lowest interest rate. Start by listing all of your debts in order from highest interest rate to lowest interest rate. Make the minimum payment on each debt except for the debt with the highest interest rate. On the debt with the highest interest rate, pay as much as you can afford each month until it is paid off. Once the debt with the highest interest rate is paid off, move on to the debt with the next highest interest rate and repeat the process.

Both the debt snowball and debt avalanche methods have their advantages and disadvantages. The debt snowball method can provide a quick win and a sense of accomplishment as you pay off your smallest debts first. However, it may not be the most financially efficient method since you may end up paying more interest over time. The debt avalanche method, on the other hand, may take longer to see progress, but it can save you more money in the long run since you are paying off the debts with the highest interest rates first.

Regardless of which method you choose, it's important to have a plan and stick to it. Here are some tips to help you successfully implement a debt payoff strategy:

1. Create a budget: In order to pay off your debts, you need to know where your money is going. Create a budget that includes all of your income and expenses,

and identify areas where you can cut back on spending.

2. Make a plan: Choose the debt payoff method that works best for you and create a plan. Determine how much you can afford to pay each month and how long it will take you to pay off each debt.

3. Stay motivated: Paying off debt can be a long and difficult process. Stay motivated by tracking your progress and celebrating small wins along the way.

4. Avoid new debt: It's important to avoid taking on new debt while you are paying off your existing debt. Cut up your credit cards, avoid taking out loans, and focus on living within your means.

5. Seek help if needed: If you are struggling to pay off your debts or need additional support, consider reaching out to a financial advisor or credit counseling service for assistance.

Paying off debt can be a challenging process, but it is an important step towards achieving financial stability and freedom. By using a debt payoff strategy such as the debt snowball or debt avalanche method, you can prioritize your debts and work towards becoming debt-free.

Learn about investing.

Assuming you are free of debt, and you have money to put aside, we want to tackle investing this money. To put this into a small subchapter seems somewhat ironic because investing is such a huge topic that is not learned by reading a few paragraphs. However, I want to give a short summary as we are about to take a step over to the next chapter.

Investing is the process of using money to earn a return or profit. It is a key aspect of personal finance, and those who invest their money wisely can potentially build significant wealth over time. However, for many people, investing can be intimidating and confusing. It requires a basic understanding of financial markets, investment vehicles, and risk management. In this chapter, we will explore the basics of investing and provide tips on how to get started.

The first step to learning about investing is understanding the concept of risk and return. Generally speaking, higher returns come with higher risk. Investors who are willing to take on more risk may be able to earn higher returns, but they also face the potential for larger losses. Conversely, investors who are risk-averse may be more comfortable with lower returns, but they also have a lower risk of losing money.

Next, it's important to understand the various investment options available to you. Some of the most common investment vehicles include stocks, bonds, mutual funds, and exchange-traded funds (ETFs). Each of these has its own unique characteristics, advantages, and risks.

Stocks are ownership stakes in a company. When you buy a stock, you become a shareholder in that company and may be entitled to a portion of its profits. However, stocks can be volatile and their prices can fluctuate rapidly based on a variety of factors such as market conditions, company performance, and global events.

Bonds, on the other hand, are debt instruments. When you buy a bond, you are essentially loaning money to a company or government. In return, you receive regular interest payments and the return of your principal investment when the bond matures. Bonds are generally considered less risky than stocks, but they also typically offer lower returns.

Mutual funds and ETFs are investment vehicles that allow investors to pool their money together to purchase a diversified portfolio of stocks, bonds, or other assets. This diversification can help reduce risk while still offering the potential for growth. Mutual funds are managed by professional fund managers who make investment decisions on behalf of the fund's investors. ETFs, on the other hand, are traded on an exchange like a stock and are designed to track a specific market index or sector.

Once you have a basic understanding of the different types of investments, it's important to create an investment plan that aligns with your goals and risk tolerance. This plan should outline your investment goals, the types of investments you want to make, and your investment time horizon. It should also take into account your overall financial situation, including your income, expenses, debt, and savings.

One important aspect of investing is diversification. This means spreading your investments across different asset classes and industries to help reduce risk. By diversifying your portfolio, you can potentially lower the impact of market volatility on your overall investment returns.

Another important consideration when investing is fees. All investments come with fees, such as management fees or trading fees. These fees can eat into your investment returns over time, so it's important to understand them and choose investments with lower fees whenever possible.

In addition to understanding the basics of investing, it's also important to stay informed about the markets and the economy. This can help you make more informed investment decisions and adjust your investment plan as needed. Regularly reviewing your portfolio and rebalancing your investments can also help ensure that your portfolio remains aligned with your goals and risk tolerance over time.

In conclusion, investing can be a powerful tool for building wealth over time, but it requires a basic understanding of financial markets, investment vehicles, and risk management. By learning about the different types of investments, creating an investment plan, diversifying your portfolio, and staying informed about the markets, you can potentially achieve your investment goals and build a more secure financial future.

# Chapter 4 - Saving and Investing

The importance of saving and investing cannot be overstated when it comes to building wealth and achieving financial freedom. Saving and investing allows you to put your hard-earned money to work for you, generating more wealth and providing financial security for the future.

Saving and investing may seem overwhelming or intimidating, but it is important to remember that every journey begins with a single step. Whether you are just starting out on your financial journey or have been managing your finances for years, there are always new tips and strategies to help you save more, invest smarter, and achieve your financial goals.

In this chapter, we will explore the importance of saving and investing, different ways to save and invest, and strategies for maximizing your savings and investments. We will also discuss common mistakes to avoid and tips for staying on track with your savings and investment goals.

The world of personal finance can be complex, but with the right knowledge and strategies, you can navigate it successfully and achieve financial freedom. So, let's get started on the journey to saving and investing for a brighter financial future.

## Save a percentage of your income.

Saving a percentage of your income is one of the most important financial habits you can develop. It allows you to build wealth, create an emergency fund, and reach your financial goals faster. Unfortunately, many people struggle with saving money, and as a result, they live paycheck to paycheck, accumulate debt, and have little to no savings. In this chapter, we will discuss the benefits of saving a percentage of your income, as well as practical tips for making it a habit.

The first step to saving money is to make it a priority. Many people spend their money impulsively without thinking about the long-term consequences of their actions. By setting aside a percentage of your income, you can ensure that you are living within your means and building a solid financial foundation. This means that you will have money set aside for unexpected expenses, emergencies, and future goals such as buying a house, starting a business, or retiring.

One common rule of thumb is to save at least 20% of your income, but this may not be realistic for everyone. If you are living paycheck to paycheck, it may be challenging to save that much money right away. However, any amount you can save is better than nothing. You can start by saving a smaller percentage, such as 5% or 10%, and gradually increase it over time. The key is to be consistent and make saving a habit.

Another way to make saving a percentage of your income easier is to automate it. Many banks offer automatic savings plans, which allow you to set up regular transfers from your checking account to your savings account. This means that you won't have to remember to transfer money manually, and you won't be tempted to spend the money on something else. You can also set up automatic contributions to your retirement accounts, such as a 401(k) or IRA, which will help you save for the future.

In addition to automating your savings, you can also look for ways to cut back on your expenses. This will free up more money that you can put towards your savings goals. For example, you can reduce your monthly bills by negotiating with service providers or canceling subscriptions that you don't use. You can also save money on groceries by meal planning and buying in bulk, or by using coupons and shopping at discount stores.

Another way to save money is to avoid lifestyle inflation. This is when your expenses increase as your income goes up, which can prevent you from making progress towards your financial goals. Instead of upgrading your lifestyle every time you get a raise, consider putting the extra money towards your savings or debt repayment goals. This will help you reach your financial goals faster and avoid the stress of living paycheck to paycheck.

Finally, it's important to have a plan for your savings. You should have specific goals in mind for what you want to achieve with your savings, whether it's an emergency fund, a down payment on a house, or retirement savings. Having a plan will help you stay motivated and focused on your goals. You can also track your progress and celebrate your successes along the way.

In conclusion, saving a percentage of your income is a critical financial habit that will help you build wealth, create financial security, and achieve your goals. By making saving a priority, automating your savings, cutting back on expenses, avoiding lifestyle inflation, and having a plan, you can develop a strong savings habit that will benefit you for years to come. Remember, every little bit counts, so start small and build up over time. With dedication and consistency, you can achieve financial freedom and enjoy the peace of mind that comes with knowing you have a solid financial foundation.

Build an emergency fund.

An emergency fund is a safety net that can help you avoid financial disaster when unexpected expenses or emergencies arise. These can include car repairs, medical bills, job loss, or any other unexpected expenses that require you to dip into your savings. Building an emergency fund can be the difference between staying afloat during a tough time and having to rely on credit cards or loans with high interest rates to get by.

So, how do you build an emergency fund? The first step is to determine how much money you need to set aside. Financial experts recommend having at least three to six months' worth of living expenses saved up in case of an emergency. This means you need to calculate your average monthly expenses and multiply that amount by the number of months you want to save for. For example, if your monthly expenses are $3,000, you should aim to save at least $9,000 to $18,000 for emergencies.

Once you have set your savings goal, it's time to start saving. The best way to do this is to automate your savings by setting up a direct deposit from your paycheck into a separate savings account dedicated to your emergency fund. You can also set up automatic transfers from your checking account into your emergency fund account on a regular basis. By automating your savings, you won't have to rely on willpower to save money. The money will be automatically moved out of your checking account before you even have a chance to spend it.

Another way to build your emergency fund is to cut back on unnecessary expenses. Look for ways to reduce your spending, such as cutting back on eating out, cancelling subscription services you don't use, and shopping for deals on your regular expenses. Every dollar you save can be put towards your emergency fund.

It's important to keep your emergency fund separate from your other savings accounts, such as retirement or vacation savings. This will help you resist the temptation to dip into your emergency fund for non-emergency expenses. Consider opening a high-yield savings account or a money market account for your emergency fund to earn a higher interest rate than a traditional savings account.

Remember that building an emergency fund takes time and commitment. It's not something that can be built overnight. Start small and aim to save a percentage of your income each month. Even saving $50 or $100 a month can add up over time. The key is to make saving for emergencies a priority and to be consistent with your savings efforts.

Having an emergency fund in place can provide peace of mind and financial security. You never know when unexpected expenses will arise, and having a financial cushion can help you weather the storm. By setting a savings goal, automating your savings, cutting back on unnecessary expenses, and keeping your emergency fund separate from your other savings accounts, you can build a strong emergency fund that will serve as a safety net for you and your family.

Set a savings goal and work towards it.

Setting a savings goal is a crucial step towards achieving financial stability and security. Whether it's saving up for a down payment on a house, a dream vacation, or an emergency fund, having a specific goal in mind can help you stay motivated and focused on your financial objectives.

Here are some steps to help you set a savings goal and work towards achieving it:

1. Determine your objective: The first step in setting a savings goal is to determine what you want to save for. Your goal should be specific, measurable, achievable, relevant, and time-bound (SMART). For instance, you might want to save up $10,000 for a down payment on a house in the next two years.

2. Calculate how much you need to save: Once you have a specific goal in mind, you need to figure out how much money you need to save to achieve it. This will require some research and calculations to determine how much you'll need to save each month to reach your goal within your desired timeframe.

3. Create a budget: A budget is a plan for how you'll allocate your income towards various expenses and goals. To work towards your savings goal, you'll need

to make some adjustments to your budget to ensure that you're setting aside enough money each month to reach your target.

4. Automate your savings: One of the easiest ways to save money is to make it automatic. Set up an automatic transfer from your checking account to a savings account on a regular basis, such as every payday. This will help you save consistently without having to think about it.

5. Stay motivated: Saving money can be challenging, especially if you're working towards a long-term goal. To stay motivated, try visualizing the end result of achieving your goal, such as owning your dream home or taking a once-in-a-lifetime trip. You can also break your goal into smaller milestones and celebrate each achievement along the way.

6. Track your progress: It's important to track your progress towards your savings goal regularly. This will help you identify any areas where you might be overspending and adjust your budget accordingly. It will also help you see how far you've come and stay motivated to keep going.

7. Reevaluate and adjust: As your financial situation changes, you may need to reevaluate your savings goal and adjust your plan accordingly. For instance, if you

receive a promotion or a raise, you might be able to increase your savings rate and reach your goal faster.

In conclusion, setting a savings goal is an important step towards achieving financial stability and security. By following these steps, you can create a plan to save money and work towards your financial objectives. Remember, saving money is a journey, not a destination, and it requires consistency, discipline, and patience. With time and effort, you can achieve your savings goals and build a secure financial future.

Automate your savings.

Saving money can be challenging, especially if you have to remember to set aside funds every month. But thanks to technology, it's now easier than ever to save without having to think about it. One of the best ways to do this is by automating your savings.

Automating your savings means that a portion of your income is automatically transferred into your savings account on a regular basis. This is a great way to build your savings without having to actively think about it. Here are some benefits of automating your savings:

1. Consistency: Automating your savings ensures that you save money on a regular basis, without having to remember to do it. This consistency will help you build your savings over time.

2. Discipline: By automating your savings, you are building discipline and making it a habit to save money regularly. This will help you develop a good savings habit that will last a lifetime.

3. Easy to track: When you automate your savings, it's easy to track how much you're saving each month. This can help you stay on track towards your savings goals.

4. Less temptation to spend: When the money is automatically transferred into your savings account, you're less likely to spend it. This can help you resist the urge to splurge on unnecessary purchases.

Here are some steps to take to automate your savings:

1. Set up automatic transfers: Speak to your bank or financial institution about setting up an automatic transfer from your checking account into your savings account on a regular basis. You can choose the amount and frequency of the transfer.

2. Determine how much to save: Determine how much you want to save each month and adjust your automatic transfer accordingly. Consider your income, expenses, and financial goals when setting this amount.

3. Choose the right account: Make sure you choose a savings account that offers a good interest rate and doesn't charge high fees. Look for accounts with features such as no minimum balance requirements and no monthly maintenance fees.

4. Monitor your savings: Keep an eye on your savings account to ensure that the automatic transfer is working correctly and that you're on track towards your savings goals. You may also want to review your

savings strategy periodically to ensure that it still aligns with your financial goals.

5. Adjust as necessary: If your financial situation changes, such as if you get a raise or experience a drop in income, you may need to adjust your automatic transfer accordingly.

In conclusion, automating your savings is a great way to build your savings without having to actively think about it. By setting up automatic transfers, you can save money consistently, develop good savings habits, and resist the urge to spend.

Learn about and open up an investment account.

Investing is an important part of building long-term wealth and achieving financial goals. However, many people are intimidated by the idea of investing, and may not know where to start. One of the first steps towards investing is to research and open up an investment account. In this chapter, we will discuss the important things to consider when opening an investment account, and provide tips for researching and selecting the best account for your needs.

The first step towards opening an investment account is to determine what type of account you need. There are many different types of investment accounts, including brokerage accounts, retirement accounts, and education savings accounts. Each type of account has different rules and regulations, so it is important to do your research and choose the right account for your needs.

If you are interested in investing for retirement, you may want to consider opening a retirement account such as an IRA (Individual Retirement Account) or a 401(k) through your employer. These accounts offer tax benefits and are specifically designed for long-term investing. If you are interested in investing for other financial goals, such as buying a house or paying for your children's education, you may want to consider opening a brokerage account or a specific type of education savings account.

Once you have determined what type of account you need, it is important to research and compare different investment firms and brokers. Look for firms that have a good reputation, low fees, and a wide range of investment options. You may also want to consider the level of customer service and support offered by the firm, as well as any additional tools or resources that are available to help you make informed investment decisions.

When comparing investment firms and brokers, be sure to pay attention to the fees and charges associated with each account. Fees can significantly impact your investment returns over time, so it is important to choose a firm with low fees and charges. Look for firms that offer no-fee or low-fee accounts, and be sure to understand any additional charges for trades, account maintenance, or other services.

Another important consideration when opening an investment account is the level of risk you are comfortable with. Different types of investments carry different levels of risk, and it is important to choose investments that align with your risk tolerance and investment goals. If you are new to investing, you may want to start with low-risk investments such as bonds or index funds, and gradually increase your level of risk as you become more comfortable with the market.

When opening an investment account, it is also important to understand the different investment options available to you. Some investment accounts may offer a limited number of investment options, while others may provide a wide range of stocks, bonds, mutual funds, and other investment vehicles. Be sure to research and understand the different types of investments available to you, and choose investments that align with your investment goals and risk tolerance.

Finally, it is important to be patient and disciplined when investing. Investing is a long-term strategy, and it may take time to see significant returns on your investment. Avoid making impulsive investment decisions based on short-term market fluctuations, and focus on building a diversified portfolio of investments that align with your financial goals.

In conclusion, opening an investment account is an important step towards building long-term wealth and achieving financial goals. When choosing an investment account, be sure to research and compare different investment firms and brokers, consider fees and charges, and choose investments that align with your investment goals and risk tolerance. With patience and discipline, investing can be a powerful tool for building wealth and achieving financial freedom.

Learn about different investment vehicles.

We talked in brief about this topic in the last paragraphs of the previous chapter but now we need to get into a bit more detail. Another disclaimer: This is not a book specialized on investing. I will not tell you to buy specific investment vehicles. Rather, I want to inform you what can be done with money that you have on the side.

Investing your money is a great way to grow your wealth over time. However, before you start investing, it's important to understand the different types of investment vehicles available and which ones may be best for your personal financial situation. In this chapter, we'll explore some of the most common investment vehicles and their potential benefits and risks.

1. Stocks:

Stocks are a type of investment that represent ownership in a company When you buy a stock, you become a shareholder in that company and can profit if the company's stock price increases. However, stocks also carry the risk of losing money if the company performs poorly or the market experiences a downturn. It's important to research companies and their financial performance before investing in their stock.

2. Bonds:

Bonds are a type of investment that involve lending money to a company or government entity in exchange for regular interest payments and the return of your principal investment at a specified time in the future. Bonds are generally considered less risky than stocks, but they also tend to offer lower returns.

3. Mutual funds:

A mutual fund is a collection of stocks, bonds, or other investments managed by a professional fund manager. By investing in a mutual fund, you can gain exposure to a diversified portfolio of investments without having to choose individual stocks or bonds yourself. Mutual funds can be a good option for novice investors or those who don't have the time or expertise to research individual investments.

4. Exchange-traded funds (ETFs):

ETFs are similar to mutual funds in that they represent a collection of investments. However, ETFs are traded on an exchange like individual stocks and tend to have lower fees than mutual funds. ETFs can also provide more flexibility in terms of trading and diversification.

5. Real estate:

Investing in real estate involves buying property or investing in real estate investment trusts (REITs). Real estate can provide steady income through rental properties or potential appreciation in value over time. However, real estate investments also come with risks such as market fluctuations and property maintenance costs.

6. Alternative investments:

Alternative investments are any investments that don't fall into the traditional categories of stocks, bonds, or real estate. These can include things like commodities, art, or even cryptocurrency. Alternative investments can provide diversification and potentially higher returns, but they also tend to be riskier and may require more specialized knowledge.

When deciding which investment vehicles to use, it's important to consider your financial goals, risk tolerance, and time horizon. For example, if you're investing for retirement and have a long time horizon, you may be comfortable taking on more risk in exchange for the potential for higher returns. On the other hand, if you're saving for a short-term goal like a down payment on a house, you may want to choose lower-risk investments like bonds or a high-yield savings account.

It's also important to diversify your investments across different asset classes and within each asset class to minimize your overall risk. For example, you may want to invest in a mix of stocks, bonds, and real estate to ensure that your portfolio is balanced and less vulnerable to market fluctuations.

Before investing in any investment vehicle, be sure to do your research and consult with a financial advisor if you have any questions or concerns. Investing can be a powerful tool for building wealth over time, but it's important to approach it with caution and a solid understanding of the potential risks and rewards.

Invest in a diversified portfolio.

If you decided to invest you money, it is important to know about diversification. Investing in a diversified portfolio is a key strategy for achieving long-term financial growth and stability. A diversified portfolio is a mix of different types of investments, such as stocks, bonds, and real estate, that helps reduce the risk of significant losses due to the performance of any one particular investment.

Diversification is a well-established principle in investing, and is often referred to as "not putting all your eggs in one basket". The idea is that if you spread your money across multiple investments, you'll be less vulnerable to the ups and downs of any one particular market. For example, if you have all of your money invested in stocks and the stock market experiences a significant downturn, your entire portfolio could suffer. However, if you have some of your money invested in bonds or real estate, those investments may continue to perform well even as the stock market struggles.

When building a diversified portfolio, it's important to consider a variety of factors, including risk tolerance, investment goals, and time horizon. For example, younger investors with a longer time horizon may be able to tolerate more risk and may want to focus on higher-growth investments like stocks, while older investors approaching retirement may want to focus more on income-generating investments like bonds.

Another important consideration when building a diversified portfolio is asset allocation. This refers to the percentage of your portfolio that you allocate to different types of investments. A common rule of thumb is to subtract your age from 100 to determine the percentage of your portfolio that should be invested in stocks, with the remainder invested in bonds. For example, a 30-year-old would allocate 70% of their portfolio to stocks and 30% to bonds.

It's also important to consider the geographic diversification of your portfolio. Investing in stocks and bonds from different countries and regions can help further reduce your risk by spreading your investments across a range of economies and political systems. This can also provide exposure to emerging markets, which may offer higher growth potential but also carry more risk.

When investing in a diversified portfolio, it's important to regularly review and rebalance your investments to ensure that they remain aligned with your investment goals and risk tolerance. This means selling some investments and buying others in order to maintain the desired allocation. For example, if stocks have performed well and now make up a larger percentage of your portfolio than desired, you may need to sell some stocks and buy more bonds to maintain your desired asset allocation.

In summary, investing in a diversified portfolio is an important strategy for reducing risk and achieving long-term financial growth. By spreading your investments across different types of investments and asset classes, you can help protect yourself against market downturns and benefit from growth opportunities in a range of markets. It's important to regularly review and rebalance your portfolio to ensure that it remains aligned with your investment goals and risk tolerance.

Consider the fees and charges associated with your investments.

Investing can be a great way to grow your wealth and secure your financial future. However, before you start investing, it's important to consider the fees and charges associated with your investments. These fees can eat into your returns and reduce your overall profitability. In this chapter, we'll discuss some of the fees and charges you should be aware of when investing.

The first fee to consider is the expense ratio. The expense ratio is the percentage of assets that are used to cover the costs of managing the investment. This includes things like management fees, administrative costs, and other expenses. Generally, actively managed funds will have a higher expense ratio than passively managed funds like index funds and exchange-traded funds (ETFs). While it may seem like a small percentage, even a small difference in expense ratio can add up over time and eat into your overall returns.

Another fee to consider is the front-end load or sales charge. This is a fee that is charged when you purchase a mutual fund or other investment product. The fee is usually a percentage of the amount you invest and is deducted from your initial investment. For example, if you invest $10,000 in a mutual fund with a 5% front-end load, you'll actually only be investing $9,500. This fee can be significant and should be taken into consideration when choosing an investment product.

Another fee to consider is the back-end load or redemption fee. This is a fee that is charged when you sell your shares in a mutual fund or other investment product. The fee is usually a percentage of the amount you withdraw and is deducted from your earnings. For example, if you invest $10,000 in a mutual fund with a 5% back-end load and you sell your shares after one year for $11,000, you'll only receive $10,450 after the fee is deducted. This fee can also be significant and should be taken into consideration when choosing an investment product.

In addition to these fees, it's important to consider the tax implications of your investments. Capital gains taxes are charged on the profits you make from selling your investments. The tax rate depends on how long you hold the investment before selling. Short-term capital gains, which are profits made from selling an investment held for less than a year, are taxed at your ordinary income tax rate. Long-term capital gains, which are profits made from selling an investment held for more than a year, are taxed at a lower rate. It's important to keep this in mind when choosing investments and planning your investment strategy.

When investing in mutual funds, it's important to also consider the turnover ratio. The turnover ratio is a measure of how frequently the fund manager buys and sells the securities in the fund's portfolio. A higher turnover ratio can result in higher transaction costs, which can reduce your overall returns. Additionally, frequent buying and selling can lead to short-term capital gains taxes.

When investing in stocks or other individual securities, it's important to consider the brokerage fees. These fees are charged by the broker for buying and selling the securities. They can be a flat fee or a percentage of the transaction value. It's important to shop around and compare brokerage fees to ensure you're getting the best deal.

In conclusion, there are a variety of fees and charges that you should be aware of when investing. These fees can have a significant impact on your overall returns and should be taken into consideration when choosing investment products and developing your investment strategy. It's important to do your research, read the prospectus carefully, and consult with a financial advisor if necessary to ensure you're making informed investment decisions.

Use a low-cost index fund.

Investing in the stock market can be an excellent way to grow your wealth over time, but it can also be a confusing and intimidating process, especially for new investors. With so many different investment options available, it can be difficult to know where to start.

One option that is gaining popularity among investors is investing in low-cost index funds. In this chapter, we will explore what index funds are, why they are a good investment option, and how to go about investing in them.

What is an index fund?

An index fund is a type of mutual fund or exchange-traded fund (ETF) that tracks a specific market index, such as the S&P 500 or the Nasdaq Composite. Instead of trying to beat the market by picking individual stocks, index funds aim to match the performance of the index they are tracking.

Because index funds do not require active management, they typically have lower fees and expenses than actively managed funds. This makes them an attractive investment option for investors looking to keep their costs low while still gaining exposure to the stock market.

Why are index funds a good investment option?

There are several reasons why index funds are a good investment option:

1. Low fees: As mentioned earlier, index funds typically have lower fees than actively managed funds. Over time, these lower fees can add up to significant savings for investors.

2. Diversification: By investing in an index fund, you are essentially buying a small piece of every company in the index. This provides diversification, which helps to spread your risk across multiple companies and reduces the impact of any one company's performance on your portfolio.

3. Consistent returns: While index funds are not immune to market fluctuations, they tend to provide more consistent returns over time than individual stocks. This is because they are not subject to the same volatility that can occur with individual stocks.

How to invest in a low-cost index fund

Investing in a low-cost index fund is a relatively straightforward process. Here are the steps to follow:

1. Determine your investment goals: Before investing in an index fund, it is important to determine your investment goals. This will help you choose the right type of index fund to invest in and determine how much money to invest.

2. Choose the index fund: There are many different index funds available, each tracking a different market index. Do your research and choose an index fund that aligns with your investment goals.

3. Open an investment account: To invest in an index fund, you will need to open an investment account with a brokerage firm or investment company. Many online brokers offer low-cost index funds, so be sure to shop around for the best deal.

4. Invest your money: Once you have opened your investment account, you can begin investing in the index fund of your choice. Be sure to follow the instructions provided by your broker or investment company to ensure that your investment is properly allocated.

5. Monitor your investment: It is important to regularly monitor your investment to ensure that it is performing as expected. While index funds are typically less volatile than individual stocks, they can still experience fluctuations in value.

## Conclusion

Investing in a low-cost index fund can be an excellent way to gain exposure to the stock market while keeping your costs low. By investing in an index fund, you can benefit from diversification, consistent returns, and low fees.

# Chapter 5 – Miscellaneous Financial Habits

In this chapter we will discuss several (partly somewhat exotic) habits that don't quite fit into one of the previous chapters. Nevertheless, these habits can also have significant impact on your financial mindset and success.

Don't hesitate to negotiate your salary or rise.

Negotiating your salary or a raise can be a daunting task, but it is an important step in ensuring that you are being compensated fairly for your skills and contributions. Many people feel uncomfortable negotiating, but by doing so, you can potentially increase your earnings and improve your financial situation. In this chapter, we will discuss some tips and strategies for negotiating your salary or a raise.

First, it is important to do your research and understand what is considered a fair salary or raise for your position and industry. You can use online resources such as Glassdoor or Payscale to research salaries for similar positions in your area. You can also talk to colleagues or mentors in your industry to get a better understanding of what is typical for your field.

Once you have done your research and have a better understanding of what is considered fair, it is important to practice your negotiation skills. Role-playing with a friend or family member can be a helpful way to prepare for a negotiation. You can also research negotiation techniques and practice them in a low-stakes environment, such as when purchasing a car or negotiating a bill.

When negotiating your salary or a raise, it is important to be confident and assertive, but also respectful and professional. Start by expressing your interest in the position or company and highlighting your accomplishments and contributions. Then, make a clear and reasonable request for the salary or raise that you are seeking.

It is also important to be open to compromise and to listen to the employer's perspective. If they are unable to meet your salary or raise request, ask if there are other benefits or perks that could be offered instead. This could include additional vacation time, flexible hours, or a performance bonus.

In some cases, your employer may not be willing or able to meet your salary or raise request. If this is the case, it is important to consider your options. You may need to evaluate whether the job is worth staying in if you are not being compensated fairly. Alternatively, you could explore other job opportunities that offer better pay or benefits.

Another important consideration when negotiating your salary or a raise is timing. Timing can be a critical factor in whether or not your negotiation is successful. For example, it may be more difficult to negotiate a raise during a company-wide budget cut or when the company is struggling financially. On the other hand, if you have just completed a major project or received a promotion, this may be a good time to negotiate a higher salary.

It is also important to be aware of any company policies or guidelines regarding salary negotiations. Some companies may have a formal process for requesting a raise, while others may not. Be sure to familiarize yourself with your company's policies and procedures before starting the negotiation process.

In conclusion, negotiating your salary or a raise can be a nerve-wracking process, but it is an important step in ensuring that you are being compensated fairly for your work. By doing your research, practicing your negotiation skills, and approaching the negotiation with confidence and professionalism, you can increase your chances of success. Remember to be open to compromise and to consider timing and company policies when negotiating.

Take advantage of employer-sponsored retirement plans.

As you plan for your financial future, one important factor to consider is your retirement. Depending solely on your Social Security benefits may not provide you with the comfortable retirement you desire. One way to maximize your retirement savings is to take advantage of an employer-sponsored retirement plan, such as a 401(k) or 403(b).

These plans allow you to contribute a portion of your pre-tax income into a retirement savings account, which is then invested and grows tax-deferred until you withdraw the funds in retirement. In addition, many employers offer a matching contribution up to a certain percentage, which is essentially free money that can help boost your retirement savings even more.

Here are some tips for making the most of your employer-sponsored retirement plan:

1. Understand your plan: Before you start contributing to your employer-sponsored retirement plan, take the time to understand the plan's rules and investment options. Review the plan's Summary Plan Description (SPD), which outlines the plan's features, eligibility requirements, and investment options. If you have

questions, don't hesitate to ask your employer's human resources department or a financial advisor.

2. Contribute as much as possible: Aim to contribute the maximum amount allowed by your plan each year. The IRS sets contribution limits each year, which may vary based on your age and income level. For 2021, the contribution limit for a 401(k) plan is $19,500 for individuals under age 50, and $26,000 for those age 50 and over.

3. Take advantage of employer matching: Many employers offer a matching contribution, up to a certain percentage of your salary. For example, your employer may match 50% of your contributions, up to 6% of your salary. This means that if you contribute 6% of your salary to your retirement plan, your employer will contribute an additional 3%. Be sure to contribute at least enough to take advantage of this free money.

4. Consider the Roth option: Many employer-sponsored retirement plans now offer a Roth option, which allows you to contribute after-tax dollars to your retirement account. While you won't get an immediate tax break, your contributions and earnings will grow tax-free, and you won't have to pay taxes on your withdrawals in retirement. This can be particularly

beneficial if you expect to be in a higher tax bracket in retirement.

5. Rebalance your portfolio regularly: Over time, your investment portfolio may become unbalanced as certain assets perform better than others. Rebalancing your portfolio involves selling some investments and buying others to maintain your desired asset allocation. Many retirement plans offer automatic rebalancing, but you may also choose to do it manually.

6. Review your plan regularly: It's important to regularly review your retirement plan to ensure that you're on track to meet your goals. Make any necessary adjustments to your contributions or investment choices to stay on course.

7. Don't cash out early: If you leave your job, you may be tempted to cash out your retirement savings. However, this can be a costly mistake, as you'll likely face taxes and penalties for early withdrawal. Instead, consider rolling over your retirement savings into an IRA or your new employer's retirement plan.

In summary, an employer-sponsored retirement plan can be a powerful tool for building your retirement savings. By contributing as much as possible, taking advantage of employer matching, considering the Roth option, regularly rebalancing your portfolio, and reviewing your plan regularly, you can ensure that you're on track to achieve your retirement goals.

Review your insurance policies to make sure you have adequate coverage.

When it comes to financial planning, insurance is an essential aspect that one cannot overlook. Insurance protects us against unforeseen circumstances that may have a severe impact on our finances. However, the cost of insurance can be a significant drain on our finances, and as such, it's crucial to review our policies periodically to ensure we have adequate coverage and to cut any unnecessary bills. In this chapter, we will discuss the importance of reviewing your insurance policies and how to cut down on unnecessary bills.

One of the first steps towards ensuring that you have adequate coverage and reducing your insurance bills is by understanding your insurance policies. Take time to read through your insurance policies, including your health insurance, auto insurance, home insurance, and life insurance policies. Make sure that you understand the coverage, limitations, and exclusions of each policy. If you find any aspects of the policies confusing, reach out to your insurance agent for clarification. Understanding your policies is critical as it will help you make informed decisions about the coverage you need, and help you avoid paying for coverage you don't need.

The next step is to review your insurance needs periodically. As we go through life, our insurance needs change, and it's essential to adjust our coverage accordingly. For instance, if you recently purchased a new car or home, you may need to increase your auto or home insurance coverage. Similarly, if you have a growing family, you may need to review your life insurance coverage. Reviewing your insurance needs will help you ensure that you have adequate coverage and avoid paying for coverage you don't need.

One way to reduce your insurance bills is by bundling your insurance policies. Many insurance providers offer a discount when you bundle multiple policies with them. For instance, if you have auto insurance and home insurance policies with the same provider, you may be eligible for a discount. Bundling your policies can help you save money on your insurance bills while still ensuring that you have adequate coverage.

Another way to reduce your insurance bills is by increasing your deductibles. A deductible is the amount you pay out of pocket before your insurance coverage kicks in. The higher your deductible, the lower your insurance premium. However, be sure to choose a deductible that you can afford to pay out of pocket in case of a claim.

It's also essential to review your insurance policies periodically to cut any unnecessary bills. For instance, if you have an auto insurance policy for an old car that you rarely use, it may be time to consider canceling the policy. Similarly, if you have a life insurance policy with a high premium that you no longer need, you may want to consider canceling it.

When it comes to health insurance, it's essential to review your coverage and costs carefully. If you have a high-deductible health plan, consider opening a health savings account (HSA). An HSA is a tax-advantaged account that allows you to save money for medical expenses. Contributions to an HSA are tax-deductible, and withdrawals for qualified medical expenses are tax-free.

Finally, consider shopping around for insurance policies to ensure that you are getting the best deal. Compare insurance quotes from multiple providers to find the coverage that meets your needs at a reasonable cost. Be sure to check the reputation and financial stability of any insurance provider you are considering ensuring that they will be able to pay claims if necessary.

In conclusion, reviewing your insurance policies is an essential aspect of financial planning. It's crucial to understand your policies, review your insurance needs periodically, bundle your policies, increase your deductibles, cut any unnecessary bills, and shop around for insurance policies to ensure that you are getting the best deal. By following these tips, you can reduce your insurance bills while still ensuring that you have adequate coverage.

Invest in yourself by learning new skills or obtaining a certification.

Investing in oneself is one of the most significant investments an individual can make. In today's rapidly changing world, it is essential to learn new skills and obtain certifications to stay relevant in one's profession or to explore new career opportunities. Investing in oneself can lead to personal and professional growth, increased job satisfaction, and higher earning potential. In this chapter, we will explore how to invest in oneself by learning new skills or obtaining a certification.

The first step to investing in oneself is to identify the skills or certifications that are in demand in one's field. Researching job postings or speaking with professionals in the industry can help to identify these skills or certifications. Once identified, it is essential to assess one's current skillset and identify areas that need improvement. This assessment can help to identify the most effective learning opportunities and ensure that one is investing in the right skills or certifications.

One of the most accessible ways to learn new skills is through online courses or webinars. There are numerous websites, such as Coursera, edX, and Udemy, that offer affordable courses in a variety of fields. These courses are often self-paced and can be completed at any time, making them ideal for those with busy schedules. Some courses also offer certificates of completion, which can be added to a resume or LinkedIn profile to demonstrate one's skills to potential employers.

Another way to invest in oneself is to attend conferences or workshops related to one's field. These events offer the opportunity to learn from industry experts, network with professionals in the field, and stay up-to-date with the latest industry trends. While attending these events may require travel expenses, the knowledge gained can be invaluable and lead to increased job opportunities or higher earning potential.

Obtaining a certification is another way to invest in oneself. Certifications demonstrate to potential employers that an individual has the necessary skills and knowledge to excel in a particular field. They can also lead to higher salaries and increased job opportunities. Certifications are available in a wide range of fields, including IT, finance, project management, and healthcare. Researching the certifications that are most in demand in one's field and investing in obtaining them can lead to significant career growth.

Investing in oneself can also involve seeking out a mentor or joining a professional association. Mentors can offer guidance and advice based on their experiences in the industry. Professional associations often offer networking opportunities, access to job postings, and resources to help members stay up-to-date with industry trends. Joining a professional association can help to connect with other professionals in the industry and lead to valuable career opportunities.

In addition to learning new skills and obtaining certifications, investing in oneself can also involve taking care of one's physical and mental health. Exercise, healthy eating habits, and stress management techniques can lead to increased productivity and overall well-being. Investing in one's health can also reduce healthcare costs in the long run and ensure that one is able to perform at their best in their personal and professional life.

Finally, investing in oneself can also involve taking risks and stepping outside of one's comfort zone. This may involve taking on new challenges at work or pursuing a passion project outside of work. Taking risks can lead to personal and professional growth, increased confidence, and the development of new skills.

In conclusion, investing in oneself is a critical component of personal and professional growth. Learning new skills, obtaining certifications, attending conferences, seeking out a mentor, and taking care of one's physical and mental health are all ways to invest in oneself. By investing in oneself, individuals can increase their earning potential, job satisfaction, and overall well-being. It is never too late to invest in oneself and take the next step towards personal and professional growth.

Invest in a college savings plan for your children's education.

Investing in a college savings plan for your children's education can be one of the most important financial decisions you make as a parent. College education is a significant investment, and with the rising costs of tuition, it's never too early to start saving.

The first step in investing in a college savings plan is to understand what it is and how it works. A college savings plan is a type of investment account that is designed to help parents save for their children's education. These plans are also known as 529 plans, named after the section of the tax code that governs them.

529 plans offer several benefits that make them an attractive option for parents looking to save for their children's education. First and foremost, they offer tax advantages. Contributions to a 529 plan grow tax-free, and withdrawals used for qualified education expenses, such as tuition, room and board, and textbooks, are also tax-free.

There are two types of 529 plans: prepaid tuition plans and college savings plans. Prepaid tuition plans allow you to lock in the cost of tuition at a participating college or university.

College savings plans, on the other hand, allow you to invest in a variety of mutual funds or exchange-traded funds (ETFs) to help grow your savings over time.

When investing in a college savings plan, it's important to choose the right plan for your family's needs. There are many different 529 plans available, and each has its own set of fees, investment options, and rules. You'll want to consider factors such as the plan's performance history, investment options, fees, and the state tax benefits available.

One thing to keep in mind is that you're not limited to investing in your own state's 529 plan. In fact, you may find that another state's plan offers better investment options or lower fees. It's important to do your research and compare different plans before making a decision.

Another consideration when investing in a college savings plan is how much to contribute. While it's important to start saving as early as possible, it's also important to balance your college savings with other financial goals, such as retirement savings or paying off debt. A financial advisor can help you determine a savings strategy that works for your family's unique situation.

Once you've chosen a college savings plan and determined how much to contribute, the next step is to set up automatic contributions. Most plans offer the option to set up automatic contributions, which can make saving for college easier and more convenient.

It's important to review your college savings plan periodically and make adjustments as needed. This may include changing your investment options or increasing your contributions. It's also important to keep in mind that your child's education goals may change over time, so it's a good idea to remain flexible and adjust your plan accordingly.

In addition to investing in a college savings plan, there are other ways to help pay for college. Your child may be eligible for scholarships, grants, or other forms of financial aid. It's important to explore all of your options and develop a comprehensive plan to pay for college.

Investing in a college savings plan for your children's education can be a smart financial decision that helps set them up for success. By doing your research, choosing the right plan, and contributing regularly, you can help ensure that your child has the financial resources they need to pursue their education and achieve their goals.

Use a credit monitoring service to keep track of any fraudulent activity.

Whether you are applying for a loan, trying to rent an apartment, or applying for a job, your credit score and history can have a significant impact on your financial future. Unfortunately, identity theft and credit fraud have become increasingly common, leaving many people vulnerable to financial harm. This is where credit monitoring services come in.

Credit monitoring services are designed to keep track of your credit history and alert you to any changes or fraudulent activity. These services can be an essential tool for protecting your credit and preventing identity theft. In this chapter, we will discuss the benefits of using a credit monitoring service and how to choose the right one for your needs.

Firstly, credit monitoring services can provide you with peace of mind by constantly monitoring your credit report and alerting you to any suspicious activity. This includes new credit applications, changes in your credit score, and any new accounts opened in your name. With a credit monitoring service, you can quickly identify and respond to any fraudulent activity, preventing long-term financial damage.

Secondly, credit monitoring services can also help you improve your credit score. By keeping track of your credit history and alerting you to any errors or inaccuracies, you can quickly correct any issues that may be negatively impacting your credit score. Additionally, some credit monitoring services offer personalized recommendations for improving your credit score, such as paying down credit card balances or disputing inaccurate information.

When choosing a credit monitoring service, there are a few factors to consider. Firstly, it's important to choose a reputable service with a proven track record of providing accurate and timely alerts. Look for a service that offers real-time alerts and has a user-friendly platform for monitoring your credit history.

Secondly, consider the cost of the service. Some credit monitoring services are free, while others charge a monthly or annual fee. While free services may seem like a good option, they often have limited features and may not provide the same level of protection as paid services. It's essential to weigh the cost of the service against the potential cost of identity theft or credit fraud.

Thirdly, look for a credit monitoring service that offers additional features, such as credit score tracking or identity theft insurance. Some services may also provide personalized credit advice or offer access to financial professionals who can answer your questions and provide guidance on managing your credit.

Finally, it's important to read the fine print and understand the terms and conditions of the credit monitoring service. Make sure you understand the scope of the service, including what types of alerts are provided and how often you will receive them. Additionally, be aware of any limitations or exclusions in the service, such as limitations on the amount of identity theft insurance coverage provided.

In conclusion, using a credit monitoring service can be an essential tool for protecting your credit and preventing identity theft. By constantly monitoring your credit report and alerting you to any suspicious activity, these services can provide you with peace of mind and help you maintain a healthy credit score. When choosing a credit monitoring service, be sure to consider the reputation of the provider, the cost of the service, additional features, and the terms and conditions of the service. With the right credit monitoring service, you can take control of your credit and protect your financial future.

Create a passive income stream.

This book is coming to an end and the topics are getting more advanced. Passive income is a term that can be found increasingly and is advertised by influencers, youtubers and on blogs all over the internet. In my opinion, there is no such thing as passive income. No matter what you plan to do, you first have to be active and invest time (and sometimes also money).

Creating a passive income stream may sound like an excellent way to build wealth and financial stability. Passive income is called the money you earn without actively working for it. Instead, you invest your time, energy, and resources upfront, and then the income comes in on autopilot. This is different from active income, where you trade time and labor for money.

There are several ways to create a passive income stream, and some options require more upfront investment than others. However, the benefits of generating passive income can be significant, including financial freedom, the ability to retire early, and more flexibility in your career and personal life.

One popular way to generate passive income is through real estate investing. Real estate has been a wealth-building strategy for centuries, and it continues to be a reliable way to create passive income. You can invest in rental properties, either residential or commercial, and earn monthly rental income. This requires upfront capital to purchase the property, as well as ongoing maintenance and management. However, with a solid investment strategy and a good property management team, real estate investing can be an excellent source of passive income.

Another way to generate passive income is through dividend investing. Dividend stocks are shares of companies that pay out a portion of their profits to shareholders. By investing in dividend-paying stocks, you can earn a regular stream of income without having to sell shares or do any additional work. It's important to research companies and their dividend histories before investing to ensure you choose stable and reliable companies that can provide consistent income.

If you're interested in generating passive income through investments but don't have the upfront capital to purchase real estate or invest in stocks, there are still options available. Crowdfunding platforms allow investors to pool their money together to invest in real estate or other ventures. This can be a great way to generate passive income while spreading the risk across multiple investments.

Another option is to create and sell digital products, such as ebooks, courses, or software. Once you've created the product, you can sell it repeatedly without needing to put in additional work. This requires upfront investment of time and resources to create the product, but once it's available for sale, it can generate passive income for years to come.

If you have a creative side, you can also generate passive income through licensing your artwork, music, or other intellectual property. This allows you to earn royalties every time your work is used or reproduced. Similarly, you can also generate passive income through affiliate marketing, where you promote products or services and earn a commission on any sales made through your referral link.

Ultimately, the key to creating a successful passive income stream is finding a strategy that works for you and fits your financial goals and lifestyle. It's important to do your research, evaluate the risks and potential rewards, and have a solid plan in place before investing your time and resources. Remember that passive income is not a get-rich-quick scheme, but rather a long-term strategy for building wealth and financial stability.

In conclusion, creating a passive income stream can be a viable way to build financial stability and generate income without trading time and labor for money. However, it also requires an active input of time and/or money. Real estate investing, dividend investing, crowdfunding, digital product creation, licensing, and affiliate marketing are all viable options for generating passive income. It's important to find a strategy that fits your financial goals and lifestyle and to have a solid plan in place before investing your time and resources. With dedication and hard work, passive income can provide financial freedom and flexibility for years to come.

# Chapter 6 - A short conclusion.

Throughout this book, we have discussed various strategies and tips for managing personal finances and achieving financial goals. The importance of having a solid financial plan cannot be overstated, as it can be the key to achieving financial security and stability.

We have touched on many different areas of personal finance, including budgeting, saving, investing, debt management, insurance, and more. One overarching theme that emerged was the need for discipline and consistency when it comes to managing finances. This involves developing good financial habits, such as tracking expenses, creating a budget, and setting financial goals.

We also highlighted the importance of being proactive and taking action when it comes to personal finance. This includes being knowledgeable about different financial products and services, researching before making major purchases, and taking advantage of employer-sponsored retirement plans.

Another key concept we discussed was the idea of investing in oneself. This can involve learning new skills or obtaining certifications to increase earning potential, as well as taking care of one's physical and mental health.

In addition, we emphasized the importance of being mindful of expenses and making informed decisions. This can involve using a cash flow projection tool, negotiating for a higher salary or better terms on loans, and being aware of fees and charges associated with financial products.

One area that cannot be overlooked is the importance of managing debt. We discussed various strategies for managing debt, including the debt snowball and debt avalanche methods, as well as paying off credit card debt in full every month. Additionally, we talked about the importance of monitoring credit scores and using credit monitoring services to prevent fraudulent activity.

Overall, the key takeaway is that personal finance is an ongoing process that requires consistent effort and attention. By developing good financial habits, being proactive, and making informed decisions, individuals can achieve financial stability and security. While there may be challenges and setbacks along the way, with persistence and determination, it is possible to reach one's financial goals and achieve financial freedom.

Small Habits, Big Rewards –
A Step-by-Step Guide to Financial Freedom

For Mary

Nathaniel Brooks
January 2023